25 More

BRIDGE CONVENTIONS

YOU

SHOULD KNOW

MASTER POINT PRESS • TORONTO

To Justin, our first grandchild, with love. *Barbara Seagram*

Master Point Press
331 Douglas Ave.
Toronto, Ontario Canada
M5M 1H2
(416) 781-0351 Fax (416) 781-1831
Website: http://www.masterpointpress.com
Email: info@masterpointpress.com

National Library of Canada Cataloguing in Publication
Seagram, Barbara
25 more bridge conventions you should know / Barbara Seagram & David Bird.

ISBN 1-894154-65-7

1. Contract bridge--Bidding. I. Bird, David, 1946- II. Title.
III. Title: Twenty-five more bridge conventions you should know.
GV1282.4.S423 2003   795.41'52   C2003-902597-7

Editor	Ray Lee
Cover and interior design	Olena S. Sullivan/New Mediatrix
Interior format and copy editing	Deanna Bourassa & Luise Lee

Printed and bound in Canada by Webcom Canada Ltd.

2 3 4 5 6 7   *07 06 05 04*

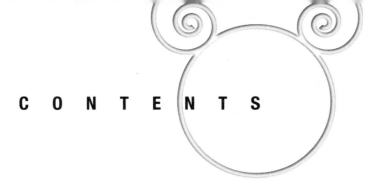

C O N T E N T S

INTRODUCTION

What is your attitude to conventions? 'Let's put as many as possible on our convention card. They're fun to play and make us look like real experts!'? Perhaps so, but playing a new convention is not as simple as putting another golf club in your bag, though. You have to make sure that your total bidding system covers, as well as possible, all the hands on which you will want to make a bid. Whenever you decide to use some particular bid in a conventional way, you must be certain that you can afford to abandon the natural use of this bid. For example, players readily took up the Stayman convention because they could see that a weak takeout into clubs (in the sequence 1NT – 2♣) was not much use, while being able to locate a 4-4 major-suit fit was really valuable.

As we describe each convention in this book, we will make it clear what you are giving up by abandoning the natural use of the bid. We will also mention the situations where one convention in the book conflicts with another. In short, our intention has been to provide you with all the information you need to decide whether or not to play the conventions we cover here. They are all popular conventions, many with a huge following around the world. Nevertheless, it is up to you to decide which of them will fit neatly into your own system.

In case you are unfamiliar with some of the terms used in bridge books, LHO is short for your left-hand opponent, the player sitting on your left. Similarly RHO is short for right-hand opponent. HCP means high-card points, on the traditional 4/3/2/1 scale. When instead we say 'points', we mean that you should add your distributional points to the total. We make no reference to the need to alert certain conventional bids in duplicate competition. That's because the rules differ from country to country, and even from club to club; the authorities also tend to modify them at three-monthly intervals! It will be up to you to find out which ones require an alert when you play.

This book leans heavily on its best-selling predecessor *25 Bridge Conventions You Should Know*. Rather than replicate information from that book, we will refer to it whenever necessary. For example, when we describe minor-suit transfers opposite 1NT, we will refer you to the first book for information on major-suit transfers.

Let the instruction and entertainment commence, then! We hope that you enjoy the book and that the conventions you choose to adopt will work well for you at the table.

Barbara Seagram and David Bird

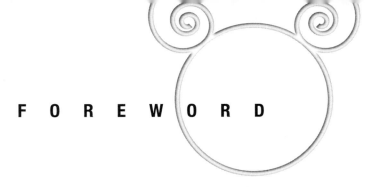

F O R E W O R D

In the early 1980s, I was a teenager who had fallen in love. My love was the game of bridge and I spent a great deal of time pursuing her at Kate Buckman's Bridge Studio, the foremost bridge club in my home city of Toronto. Like almost all new bridge players, I eagerly tried to learn as many bidding conventions as possible.

What a mistake! Learning a lot of conventions was a mistake because I did not learn about them properly. It took me over ten years to unlearn some of the bad habits that I had picked up.

When most bridge players (and I was not an exception) learn a new convention, all they concern themselves with is the basic mechanics of how that convention works. Follow-up auctions, why a convention is used, when a convention should be used (and not used) are all vital issues that are blissfully ignored by most students of our game. I learned these lessons the hard way, but thanks to this book, you don't have to!

Barbara Seagram, who managed Kate Buckman's when I played there, already had a well-deserved reputation as one of the best bridge teachers in the city. Now, twenty years later, she is widely recognized as one of North America's premier bridge teachers. She has teamed up with David Bird, one of the most popular and prolific bridge writers in the world, to produce this sensational book. Barbara's skill as a teacher combined with David's talents for writing about the game make them an ideal partnership.

This book carries on where Barbara's award-winning *25 Bridge Conventions You Should Know* left off, this time presenting a set of popular and effective conventions suitable for intermediate level players. You may have heard of most of these conventions before and you probably use some of them yourself already, but I am willing to bet that even seasoned tournament players will find a lot of food for thought in these pages.

This book has everything that a book on conventions should have – detailed explanations of the conventions themselves (many with variations), why these conventions are useful, when they should be used, example deals from major tournaments, and plenty of quizzes.

I only wish that Barbara and David had been writing books about conventions when I was an intermediate level player!

Fred Gitelman

1

LEARN THESE FIRST

C H A P T E R 1

CAPPELLETTI DEFENSE TO 1NT

W H A T ' S   I N   A   N A M E ?

 The popular Cappelletti Defense to a 1NT opening was invented by **Michael Cappelletti**. Not to be confused with his son Mike Jr. (also a well-known bridge expert), the elder Cappelletti is a leading authority on Omaha poker.

When you are deciding whether to enter the bidding against an opposing 1NT opening, does it make much difference if the 1NT is weak or strong? It sure does! When the opening is weak (12-14 points), you may well be able to make game your way. This is rarely the case against a strong 1NT. The other difference is that against a weak 1NT, most people consider it essential to have a penalty double available. Against a strong 1NT it is largely a waste of time to use a double for penalties (even if the double is based on a good suit to run, the opponents can usually escape into a long suit of their own.

In this chapter we will look at the Cappelletti Defense to 1NT. This does include a penalty double and is therefore particularly recommended for use against a weak 1NT. In Chapter 7 we will describe the D.O.N.T. defense to the strong 1NT. If you do not

BY THE WAY

The Cappelletti convention is known as 'Hamilton' west of the Mississippi, and as 'Pottage' in the UK. It must be a good convention if three different people invented it independently!

want to play two different defenses, there is nothing at all wrong with playing Cappelletti against both the strong and weak notrump. That is exactly what a vast number of players do.

So what is Cappelletti?

These are the two situations where you may want to enter the auction over a 1NT opening – second seat and fourth seat:

LHO	Partner	RHO	You
		1NT	?

LHO	Partner	RHO	You
1NT	pass	pass	?

Here are the bids that Cappelletti offers. In both the second and fourth seats you may choose between these actions:

dbl	for penalties
2♣	a single-suiter in any of the four suits
2♦	both major suits
2♥	hearts and an undisclosed minor
2♠	spades and an undisclosed minor
2NT	both minor suits

When you bid 2♦, 2♥ or 2♠ your two-suiter may be 4-5 or 5-4. This is a common feature of all defenses to 1NT that describe two-suited hands. As responder, you may sometimes have to guess which suit to choose. There is no need to worry about this. The situation is just the same as when you have to choose which suit to bid facing a takeout double. The 2NT overcall carries the bidding higher and should be based on a hand that is at least 5-5 in the minor suits.

What is the expected point range for the five bids between 2♣ and 2NT? When you hold 15 points or more against a weak 1NT, you will usually begin with a penalty double. The range for the Cappelletti bids is therefore about 9-14 points.

This is a typical hand on which you would make a Cappelletti 2♣ bid:

♠ 10 3   ♥ K Q 10 7 5 2   ♦ 9 5   ♣ K J 3

LHO	Partner	RHO	You
		1NT	?

You overcall with 2♣, showing a single-suiter somewhere. Partner will usually respond 2♦, asking you which suit you hold, and here you will rebid 2♥. If instead you held six diamonds, you would pass.

Now suppose you hold a two-suiter:

♠ A J 9 3 ♥ Q J 10 7 5 ♦ A 3 ♣ 7 4

LHO	Partner	RHO	You
		1NT	?

You would bid 2♦ to show both the major suits.

♠ K Q 10 4 ♥ J 7 ♦ A 10 9 8 5 ♣ 7 2

LHO	Partner	RHO	You
		1NT	?

Here your call would be 2♠, showing spades and a minor. What action would you take on this next hand?

♠ A Q J 3 ♥ 6 ♦ J 8 4 ♣ A K Q 7 4

LHO	Partner	RHO	You
		1NT	?

A four-card major and a five-card minor... so, does that make it another 2♠ bid? No! You should double for penalties. Remember that the suit bids are limited to a maximum of around 14 points, particularly when you are playing against a weak 1NT and would tend to double on any hand containing 15 points or more. Against a strong 1NT a penalty double is much less common and would usually be based on a hand containing a good suit to lead.

What do you do if partner doubles?

When partner doubles 1NT for penalties, you will usually pass. In particular, you should be wary of pulling the double on a balanced hand just because you are weak.

However, if you are weak and you have an escape suit at least five cards long, you are allowed to remove the double:

♠ 6 4 ♥ J 9 8 5 2 ♦ 8 5 ♣ 10 9 6 2

LHO	Partner	RHO	You
1NT	dbl	pass	?

You would bid 2♥ on this hand. Partner will realize that you are very weak and should be wary about bidding any further.

How does the bidding continue after 2♣?

When partner overcalls 2♣ he shows an unspecified suit of six cards or longer. As responder, you may take one of these actions:

pass	if you hold six or more clubs
2♦	asks partner to bid his suit
2♥/2♠	a good heart or spade suit of your own
2NT	strong (11+ points) and balanced; game is possible

Let's look at some possible hands after this start to the auction:

♠ 10   ♥ 10 8 6 3   ♦ A 9 4   ♣ K 10 9 8 2

LHO	Partner	RHO	You
1NT	2♣	pass	?

You expect partner to have a spade suit, yes, but don't pass 2♣. A 6-1 spade fit will play okay and there is no reason to expect 2♣ to be a better contract. Apart from that, it is possible that partner's suit is hearts or diamonds. So, respond 2♦ to find out which suit partner has.

♠ 10 4 2   ♥ A Q J 9 3 2   ♦ J 9 8   ♣ 2

LHO	Partner	RHO	You
1NT	2♣	pass	?

Here there is a fair chance that partner holds a club suit and that 2♥ will be a better contract than 3♣ (especially at matchpoints). You should respond 2♥ instead of 2♦.

♠ A 10 4   ♥ K J 5   ♦ A 9 4   ♣ Q 8 7 2

LHO	Partner	RHO	You
1NT	2♣	pass	?

Now there is a chance of game and you show your strength (and a balanced hand) by bidding 2NT. Partner will rebid 3NT when he is upper-range with a minor suit. When he is upper-range with a major he will bid game in his suit. On a lower-range hand, partner will sign off in three of his suit, leaving any further move to you.

What if they bid over 2♣?

When you agree to play a new convention such as this, it is important to know what to do when there is further bidding by the opponents. Suppose your partner overcalls 2♣, showing a single-suiter, and the next player doubles:

LHO	Partner	RHO	You
1NT	2♣	dbl	?

What should you do now? The most popular method is that 'Pass' says you would be happy to play in clubs and 'Redouble' asks partner to bid his suit.

What if the next player makes a bid instead?

♠ A 10 4   ♥ K J 5   ♦ 10 9 4   ♣ Q 8 7 2

LHO	Partner	RHO	You
1NT	2♣	2♠	?

Generally, a double by you is for takeout whenever (as here) you do not know partner's suit (or suits). If partner's overcall had identified his suit (or suits) a double would be for penalties. Here a double is for takeout because you do not know which suit partner holds. On the hand we have given, you are happy to compete whatever suit partner has.

It is an admitted weakness of Cappelletti that you are at a disadvantage here because you do not know partner's suit and may wish to compete if he has some suits but not if he has others. The only advice we can offer is that you must be fairly bold with your use of the takeout double. Otherwise you may lose out to those who are playing more natural methods.

How does the bidding continue after 2♦?

When your partner shows the two major suits with an overcall of 2♦, the continuations are straightforward.

LHO	Partner	RHO	You
1NT	2♦	pass	?

pass	a long diamond suit and no major-suit fit
2♥/2♠	to play
3♥/3♠	invites partner to bid game with a maximum
2NT	asks partner for more information

After the 2NT bid, partner's rebid of 3♥ or 3♠ would show 5-4 shape and a minimum hand (the major he bids is the five-carder). Similarly, a rebid of 4♥ or 4♠ would show an upper-range 5-4 hand. When he is 5-5, he bids either 3♣ (lower range) or 4♣ (upper range).

Now suppose again that the third player doubles:

LHO	Partner	RHO	You
1NT	2♦	dbl	?

As before, a pass means that you want to play in the suit that partner has bid artificially – here, diamonds. A redouble is again SOS, asking partner to bid his better major. If instead you have a clear preference for one of the majors, you bid 2♥ or 2♠.

What about this situation:

LHO	Partner	RHO	You
1NT	2♦	3♣	?

This time, since you know which suits partner holds, a double of any bid made by RHO will be for penalties.

How does the bidding continue after 2♥ or 2♠?

An overcall of 2♥ or 2♠ shows the bid suit and an unspecified minor suit. As responder you can either pass partner in two of his major, raise the major, or bid 2NT to discover which minor he holds.

Partner	You
♠ K 10 8 6 2	♠ 9
♥ A 4	♥ K 6 5
♦ A Q 7 2	♦ J 8 5 3
♣ 8 5	♣ K 10 7 6 3

LHO	Partner	RHO	You
1NT	2♠	pass	2NT
pass	3♦	all pass	

With length in both minors, you are happy to ask partner to name his minor suit. If your shape were 2-4-2-5 instead, you would pass 2♠ and keep the bidding low. Even in the worst case, where partner holds four spades and five diamonds, you will be one level lower and less likely to be doubled. Whenever partner holds five spades and four diamonds, or is 5-5, 2♠ will usually be the better spot.

Once again, do not worry that you will end up in a poor fit occasionally. It is a fact of life. The alternative is to suffer poor score after poor score, by passing and letting the 1NT bidder score well in his own contract.

As before, let's see what happens when the third player enters the auction

LHO	Partner	RHO	You
1NT	2♥	dbl	?

You can pass, as always, to play in the suit that partner has already bid. A redouble has its normal SOS meaning: it would ask partner to bid his minor suit.

Suppose next that RHO bids spades over the 2♥ overcall. How would you ask to play in partner's minor?

LHO	Partner	RHO	You
1NT	2♥	2♠	?

In this auction, a double by you asks partner to bid his minor. Remember that whenever partner's suit or suits have not been completely identified, a double by you is for takeout. Only when you already know his suit or suits is a double for penalties.

How does the bidding continue after 2NT?

An overcall of 2NT shows both minors, and implies a little more strength since the auction is forced to the three-level. The simplest method for responding to this overcall is to pretend partner has used the Unusual Notrump. If you want to brush up on this convention, refer to the previous volume in this series, *25 Bridge Coventions You Should Know*.

Summary

✓ Since Cappelletti features a penalty double, it works best against a weak 1NT opening. However, many players use it against a strong 1NT too, so they don't have to memorize two separate methods.

✓ In both the second and fourth (balancing) seats, a 2♣ overcall of a 1NT opening shows a single-suiter; 2♦ shows both majors; 2♥ shows hearts and a minor; 2♠ shows spades and a minor; 2NT shows both minors.

✓ Facing a 2♣ overcall, you can bid 2♦ to discover partner's suit. You may also respond 2♥ or 2♠ with a long suit of your own, or pass when you hold long clubs. With a good (11+) balanced hand, bid 2NT.

✓ When the third player bids over partner's 2♣ overcall, a double by you asks partner to name his suit. You should be bold with such doubles to counter Cappelletti's main disadvantage — not naming the six-card suit.

✓ Facing a 2♥ or 2♠ overcall, you can bid 2NT to discover partner's minor suit.

CAPPELLETTI DEFENSE TO 1NT

NOW TRY THESE...

1   Playing Cappelletti, what would you say on the following hands when RHO opens 1NT?

a   ♠ A 9 7 6 4   b   ♠ Q 10 9 4
    ♥ 10 7 3   ♥ A K 9 3 2
    ♦ 5   ♦ J 9 7
    ♣ A Q 8 7   ♣ 3

c   ♠ K 5   d   ♠ 8 5
    ♥ Q 6   ♥ 3
    ♦ A J 9 6 5 2   ♦ K Q 10 5 4
    ♣ J 6 3   ♣ A Q 9 7 3

e   ♠ 10 3   f   ♠ A K J 7 6 3
    ♥ K J 9 8 2   ♥ A 8 3
    ♦ A 10 9 8 2   ♦ A 8
    ♣ 9   ♣ J 6

2   On the following hands partner has overcalled 1NT with a Cappelletti 2♣. How will you respond?

a   ♠ A Q 10 8 7 2   b   ♠ —
    ♥ 7   ♥ A 10 9 4
    ♦ K 10 8   ♦ 9 8 4
    ♣ 9 6 4   ♣ K J 10 8 5 3

3   On the following hands partner has overcalled 1NT with a Cappelletti 2♦. How will you respond?

a   ♠ K J 7   b   ♠ A J 7 5
    ♥ 9 8 3   ♥ K 7 5
    ♦ 6 4 2   ♦ A 10 8 6
    ♣ 10 7 4 2   ♣ 9 3

4   On the following hands partner has overcalled 1NT with a Cappelletti 2♥. How will you respond?

a   ♠ A K 8   b   ♠ A 10 9 6 4
    ♥ 7 2   ♥ 9 8 4
    ♦ J 10 7 2   ♦ J 7 5 2
    ♣ Q 6 5 2   ♣ 6

ANSWERS

1 **a** 2♠ To show spades and a minor suit. (If you had six spades and four clubs you would treat it as a single-suiter and bid 2♣ instead.)

    b 2♦ Perfect for the bid that shows a major two-suiter.

    c 2♣ Here you have a single-suiter and show this with 2♣.

    d 2NT With only 5-5 shape you should not be much weaker than this for a 2NT bid. Bear in mind that partner must bid at the three-level.

    e 2♥ Hearts and a minor. No problem!

    f dbl Remember that you should start with a (penalty) double on most hands of 15 or more points.

2 **a** 2♦ If partner happens to hold a six-card diamond suit (or even six clubs), you will be happy to play in a 6-3 fit there. If, as expected, partner corrects to 2♥, you can bid 2♠. At matchpoints, you might prefer to respond 2♠ directly, to ensure that you play in a major suit.

    b pass You expect partner to hold spades and are quite happy to play in clubs instead.

3 **a** 2♥ Choose the lower suit when you hold equal length, especially when you have a poor hand (there is more chance of avoiding a penalty double).

    b 3♠ With eight points in partner's suits and a minor-suit ace, you are entitled to invite game with a jump response.

4 **a** 2NT With 4-4 shape in the minors, you are happy to play in partner's minor suit. Your 2NT response asks him to bid his minor at the three-level.

    b pass You are happy to play in hearts. If you mistakenly bid 2NT, partner will probably show clubs as his minor suit.

C H A P T E R

FLANNERY TWO DIAMONDS

W H A T ' S   I N   A   N A M E ?

 William Flannery, the American inventor of the Flannery 2♦, was a steamfitter and a specialist in installing sectional boilers. While this information is of no great relevance to his convention, it might win you the occasional bet in a bar!

What is the best use for an opening bid of 2♦? One possibility is to use it as a straightforward natural weak two-bid. There is nothing at all wrong with that. It's true that a weak two in diamonds is slightly less effective as a preempt than two of a major suit, but you still rob the opponents of considerable bidding space. In this chapter we will take a close look at the Flannery 2♦ opening, which has become very popular in North America. In Chapter 25 we will consider yet another possibility — the Multi 2♦.

**A Flannery 2♦ opening shows a hand of 11-15 HCP
with exactly four spades and exactly five hearts.**

You would open a Flannery 2♦ on any of these hands:

Hand 1	Hand 2	Hand 3
♠ A J 9 7	♠ Q 10 5 3	♠ K Q 6 2
♥ K Q 5 3 2	♥ A 10 9 7 3	♥ A J 9 8 4
♦ Q 10	♦ A Q 2	♦ —
♣ 9 7	♣ 4	♣ A 10 6 3

As you see, there is a big range in potential playing strength. Hand 1 has 12 HCP and is semi-flat. When you add better distribution in the minor suits, the hand improves. Hand 2 does have better distribution, but half its high cards are in short suits – the hand would be much improved with more points concentrated in spades, for example. Hand 3 is strongest of all, almost a maximum for high card points, with three excellent suits – this is the kind of hand that could make a slam opposite the right ten-count from partner.

Flannery, then, is a convention that describes a hand with specific major-suit distribution, but that can cover a fairly wide range in terms of playing strength. We can expect, then, that responder will need some conventional machinery at his disposal if he is going to make a well-informed decision about where to place the contract.

If you have not encountered Flannery before, you may think that the 5-4 heart-spade hand is rather an obscure meaning for an opening bid. We will look first at the problem the opening bid is intended to solve. Then we will see the various routes the auction may take after a 2♦ opening.

BY THE WAY

If you play the Multi 2♦ to show a weak two in either major (see Chapter 25), you can then use a 2♥ opening bid to show a Flannery-type hand. The various continuations, described in this chapter, apply just the same.

BY THE WAY

As you will see in Chapter 19, if you play a forcing 1NT response to one of a major (very common these days, especially in two-over-one systems), the problem is even worse. A 2♥ rebid would suggest a six-card suit and 2♣ or 2♦ would show at least a three-card suit. You have no good rebid. Open with a Flannery 2♦ and you bypass this problem.

Why was Flannery invented?

Suppose you open 1♥ on this hand:

♠ K Q 9 4   ♥ A J 8 5 2   ♦ 9 5   ♣ K 4

What do you rebid when partner responds 2♣? You will have to rebid either 2♥ (unattractive on such a weak five-card suit, and possibly implying a six-card suit) or 2NT (not appealing with that diamond weakness). Reversing to 2♠ would promise more strength than you have. The problem is not so bad over a 1NT response as you can simply pass. However, there's no guarantee that 1NT is the right spot.

Flannery 2♦ is a single bid that gets the awkward hand off your chest and eliminates rebid problems.

Responding to Flannery on a weak hand

When you hold a fairly weak hand in response, you will usually sign off in one of partner's majors at the two-level. Suppose you hold these cards:

♠ Q 10 4　♥ J 2　♦ 9 8 4 2　♣ A 10 8 3

Partner	You
2♦	?

You respond 2♥, preferring the 5-2 fit in hearts to the 4-3 fit in spades. The opener will nearly always pass a response of 2♥ or 2♠. He is allowed to make another move only when he has 4-5-0-4 or 4-5-4-0 shape and a maximum hand. He will do this by bidding three of his four-card minor suit.

You should not pass the opening 2♦ bid unless you have a long diamond suit and no fit at all for partner's majors. Look at this hand, for instance:

♠ K 2　♥ 10 4　♦ Q 10 7 6 3　♣ J 9 7 5

Partner	You
2♦	?

You should respond 2♥. Since you have no idea how many diamonds partner holds (if any!), it would be a considerable gamble to pass 2♦.

♠ Q 4　♥ 5　♦ K 9 8 6 4 2　♣ K 10 7 6

Partner	You
2♦	?

Here you would pass 2♦. If you had the same major-suit holdings and were 5-5 in the minors, you would have to guess what to do.

What do you do with a good hand and a fit?

When you have a fit for one of partner's majors and a hand worth an opening bid, you simply bid game:

♠ Q J 6 4　♥ A 5　♦ K 9 8 2　♣ K 10 7

Partner	You
2♦	4♠

With around 10-12 points, you can invite game by bidding your preferred major at the three-level:

♠ A 6　♥ Q 10 4　♦ A J 10 7　♣ 10 8 3 2

Partner	You
2♦	3♥

You are inviting partner to bid 4♥ if he has a maximum.

♠ K J 9 2　♥ 5　♦ Q 10 8 6　♣ A 9 7 5

Partner	You
2♦	3♠

Here you respond 3♠, once again inviting partner to continue to game.

What if you don't have a major-suit fit?

When you need to know more about the opener's hand, which is already fairly well defined, you respond 2NT. Opener's rebid will give you this further description:

Partner	You
2♦	2NT
?	

3♣	3-card club suit (4-5-1-3 shape)
3♦	3-card diamond suit (4-5-3-1 shape)
3♥	4-5-2-2 shape, 11-13 points
3♠	4-5-2-2 shape, 14-15 points
3NT	4-5-2-2 shape, 14-15, A or K in both minors
4♣	4-card club suit (4-5-0-4 shape)
4♦	4-card diamond suit (4-5-4-0 shape)

BY THE WAY

A Flannery auction inevitably tells the opponents a great deal about opener's hand. This can be a serious drawback regardless of which side plays the hand.

This looks pretty complicated, but it breaks down like this. If he is 3-1 in the minors, partner rebids his 3-card minor. If he is 4-0 in the minors, he rebids his minor suit at the four-level. If he is 2-2 in the minors, he shows his point range, bidding 3♥ or 3♠, or (rarely) 3NT with a maximum and top minor-suit cards.

Knowledge of partner's shape in the minors may help you to judge which game to bid. Suppose partner opens 2♦ and you hold this hand:

♠ Q J 2　♥ A 5　♦ 10 7 3　♣ A Q 9 7 5

You respond 2NT to ask for more information. If partner rebids 3♣, you will know that he has a singleton diamond and three-card club support. You can then bid game in clubs. If instead he rebids 3♦, showing three diamonds and one club, you will try 3NT.

The 2NT bid can be helpful even when you have a big fit for one of partner's suits. Suppose partner opens 2♦ and you are looking at:

♠ J 5　♥ K 9 7 6 4　♦ K Q 4　♣ 9 7 5

You could simply raise to 4♥ but it is more accurate to respond 2NT. If partner has three cards in diamonds, the hands will fit well and you can bid 4♥. If instead he has three clubs and only a singleton diamond opposite your ♦ K-Q-4, the hands fit poorly and you should rebid only 3♥, leaving the final move to partner. What if your partner were to rebid 3♥ opposite your 2NT, showing a minimum 5-4-2-2 hand? You would pass.

The 3♣ and 3♦ responses

♠ 4 2   ♥ 7 5   ♦ K J 3   ♣ A Q 9 7 5 3

Partner	You
2♦	3♣

When you have no major-suit fit, but hold a long minor and about 10-12 points, you are allowed to make the special response of three of your minor. Opener should bid 3NT when he has a useful holding in your minor suit, and otherwise pass. A doubleton top honor (ace, king or queen) would give him a reasonable expectation of running your suit and he would normally rebid 3NT on this holding. As is often the case, the opener may use his judgment and pass on some hands that have a fitting honor in the minor suit:

♠ K J 9 3   ♥ K Q 8 5 4   ♦ 6 3   ♣ K 7

You	Partner
2♦	3♣
?	

Suppose you open 2♦ on this rather weak hand and partner responds 3♣. It is not attractive to rebid 3NT. You have no aces and a near-minimum point-count and should therefore pass.

FLANNERY TWO DIAMONDS

✓ The Flannery 2♦ opening shows a hand with 11-15 HCP, exactly five hearts and exactly four spades.

✓ Responder may pass with a weak hand and long diamonds or sign off in one of the major suits. A jump response of 3♥ or 3♠ invites game.

✓ A 2NT response asks for further information. Opener shows a 3-card minor by rebidding 3♣ or 3♦. A rebid of 4♣ or 4♦ would show a 4-card minor. 3♥ and 3♠ rebids show 4-5-2-2 hands, minimum and maximum respectively. 3NT shows a maximum 4-5-2-2 hand with minor-suit stoppers (ace or king).

✓ A 3♣ or 3♦ response shows a six-card minor. Opener may pass but he is should bid again (usually 3NT) when he has a good fit for the minor.

FLANNERY TWO DIAMONDS

NOW TRY THESE...

1   Playing Flannery, what would you open on each of these hands?

a   ♠ A 9 6 3
    ♥ K Q 10 8 7
    ♦ A 10 7
    ♣ 8

b   ♠ A Q 7 6
    ♥ K Q J 6 4
    ♦ 8
    ♣ A 10 3

2   On the following hands your partner has opened a Flannery 2♦. How will you respond?

a   ♠ 10 2
    ♥ K 9 8
    ♦ J 9 6 2
    ♣ A 10 6 4

b   ♠ A Q 9 2
    ♥ J 6
    ♦ K 4
    ♣ 10 8 7 6 2

c   ♠ Q 5 2
    ♥ 9
    ♦ J 8 4 2
    ♣ K 10 7 6 2

d   ♠ A 5
    ♥ A Q 5
    ♦ A 9 6 2
    ♣ Q 8 7 3

3   You have opened a Flannery 2♦ on each of these hands. How will you respond to partner's 2NT enquiry bid?

a   ♠ K 8 7 3
    ♥ A Q 9 8 2
    ♦ Q 10 3
    ♣ 4

b   ♠ A J 10 2
    ♥ K Q J 7 5
    ♦ K 4
    ♣ 10 3

c   ♠ K Q 7 5
    ♥ A 10 7 6 4
    ♦ —
    ♣ K 9 6 2

d   ♠ A Q 9 6
    ♥ K 10 8 7 6
    ♦ K 5
    ♣ K 6

4   You have opened a Flannery 2♦ on each of these hands. What will you do next if partner responds 2♥?

a   ♠ A 8 7 3
    ♥ A K 8 5 4
    ♦ J 3
    ♣ K 4

b   ♠ A 9 7 2
    ♥ K Q 10 7 5
    ♦ A J 10 4
    ♣ —

ANSWERS

1 a 2♦ Yes, that was an easy one! Perfect for Flannery.

b 1♥ Your hand is too strong for Flannery. You should open 1♥, planning to reverse to 2♠ over partner's response.

2 a 2♥ With only 8 HCP you are not strong enough to invite game with a jump to 3♥.

b 3♠ Here you have 10 HCP and four-card support for partner's spades. You are worth a game-invitational jump to the three-level.

c 2♠ The best you can do is to play in the 4-3 spade fit. It's not your fault that the hands don't fit better.

d 2NT With all strong responding hands, interested in a slam, you should start by asking for further information with the 2NT inquiry bid.

3 a 3♦ This rebid shows a three-card diamond suit. If partner continues with 3♥, inviting game, you will pass.

b 3♠ With 5-4-2-2 shape you bid 3♥ with a minimum hand and 3♠ with a maximum hand. Here your 14 HCP puts you in the upper range.

c 4♣ This response shows a four-card minor and consequently a void in the other minor. You make the same bid whether you are minimum or maximum.

d 3NT With 5-4-2-2 shape, a maximum point-count and helpful stoppers in the minors, you rebid 3NT. If partner bid 2NT with a 3-2-4-4 11-count, you will have found the best contract.

4 a pass If partner could visualize a game when you held a maximum, he would not have responded with a simple 2♥. You should not therefore advance on this hand. Remember that partner may hold only two hearts.

b 3♦ The odds switch when you have 5-4-4-0 shape. Partner may be able to visualize game now on a hand that did not previously merit a game try. (Note that you bid again only when you have this shape and a maximum. Partner may be very weak, and does not guarantee three-card heart support.)

BERGEN RAISES

WHAT'S IN A NAME?

 Bergen Raises are among a number of popular conventions created by **Marty Bergen**. A tennis champion while at college, he is now a prominent bridge player and teacher, living in Florida.

For many years, the significance of having four-card support for partner's major suit received little recognition, except among experts. That was unfortunate, because the difference in playing strength between a 5-4 fit and a 5-3 fit is enormous!

When you are playing in a 5-3 fit, it is more likely that one of the defenders will hold four trumps and that you will be vulnerable to a forcing defense (where the defenders lead their best suit to reduce your trump holding and promote their own). When you are playing in a 5-4 fit there is much less chance of losing trump control. There is less chance also that the defenders can reduce dummy's ruffing value, by leading trumps. Another important benefit is that you are likely to have trumps left in both hands after you have drawn the defenders' trumps. You may have the chance to perform an 'Elimination Play'. The more you play this game, the more you realize the value of having nine trumps rather than eight — or, even better, ten trumps rather than nine.

In Chapter 13 we will explain the Law of Total Tricks. One aspect of this is that in a competitive auction you should generally be prepared to compete to the level dictated by the total number of trumps that you and your partner hold. With nine spades between you, for example, you should be prepared to compete to the nine-trick level (a contract of 3♠). Does this depend on how many points you hold? Not really! If you hold fewer points than the opponents and go down one in 3♠, you will usually find that they could have made some contract their way. If you go down two, even doubled, they could probably have made game. That's the way the Law of Total Tricks works.

So, when your partner opens 1♥ or 1♠, promising at least five cards in his suit, the Law says that you should be willing to compete to the three-level when you hold four-card support — even if you have a very weak hand!

So what are Bergen Raises?

Bergen Raises of a major-suit opening are designed to tell partner whether you hold four-card or three-card support. They also involve getting quickly to your partnership's 'Law level', thereby taking bidding space away from your opponents. This is the scheme. When partner opens 1♥, these responses show a heart fit:

2♥	a three-card raise with 6-10 points
3♣	a four-card raise with 7-9 points
3♦	a four-card limit raise with 10-12 points
3♥	a (preemptive) four-card raise with 2-6 points
4♥	a (preemptive) five-card raise with fewer than 10 points.

The responses are along the same lines opposite a 1♠ opening: 2♠ shows a three-card raise and the Bergen 3♣ and 3♦ raises show four-card raises. Raises to 3♠ and 4♠ are preemptive.

Let's see some typical responding hands, so we can practice choosing the right Bergen response. Imagine that partner has opened 1♠ and you hold:

♠ K 10 6 5   ♥ A 10 4 2   ♦ J 5 3   ♣ 8 6

Four-card support and in the 7-9 point range, so you use the weaker of the two Bergen Raises — 3♣. The 3♣ and 3♦ responses paint a very accurate picture of the responding hand, making life easy for the opener when he has to decide whether or not to bid game. Let's add a few points:

♠ A J 6 5   ♥ 9 5   ♦ Q 10 7 4   ♣ A 6 3

You are now worth the stronger of the two Bergen responses, 3♦.

What sort of hand justifies a direct (preemptive) raise of 1♠ to 3♠? Take this action when you have four-card support with six points or fewer and enough playing strength to avoid a big penalty.

♠ K 10 6 5　♥ 5　♦ 10 8 7 4 3　♣ 9 5 2

You raise 1♠ to 3♠. There is no reason whatsoever to fear going down one or two if partner does hold a minimum hand. If that happens, the chances are excellent that the opponents could have made a game somewhere. The fact that you hold at least nine trumps between you means that the Law of Total Tricks is on your side. It is very unlikely that you will get a bad result playing at the three-level, whether or not the 3♠ contract is made.

What is the purpose of carrying the bidding so high on such a weak hand? It is to make life difficult for the opponent on your left. If he risks a four-level bid, or a takeout double, he will sometimes find that your partner has a strong hand and can extract a big penalty. If instead, he takes a cautious view and passes on some reasonable values, he may miss a game. That is the whole point of preemptive bids like these. You force the opponents to gamble. Even the luckiest of gamblers do not win all the time.

BY THE WAY

Some players prefer to switch the meaning of the Bergen 3♣ and 3♦ responses. However, the way we describe is easier to remember.

How does the bidding continue after 3♣ or 3♦?

Facing your three-level response, opener will usually have a decision to make — whether to play at the three-level or the four-level. The fact that you have given him an accurate description of your hand will make this decision easier.

Suppose you open 1♠ on this collection and are playing Bergen Raises:

♠ A Q 9 6 4　♥ A 9 3　♦ K 7 3　♣ J 4

If partner responds 3♣, showing 7-9 points, you sign off in 3♠. If instead he bid 3♦, showing 10-12 points, you would rebid 4♠.

When partner has made a Bergen 3♣ or 3♦ response, you can sometimes even pass the final decision back to him by making one of the available intermediate bids. After a start of 1♠ - 3♦, you might rebid 3♥, passing the message: 'Even after hearing your wonderful Bergen response, I still cannot make up my mind whether to bid game. You decide!' Partner would then bid 3♠ with a minimum 3♦ response and 4♠ with a maximum.

The situation is different when partner makes a direct (preemptive) raise to the three-level, a start such as 1♠–3♠. He may then have very little — perhaps only 2 or 3 HCP. It will usually be right for you to pass, even when you hold several points extra for your opening bid.

When the opener is strong enough to consider a slam opposite a Bergen 3♣ or 3♦ response, he may make a cuebid at the four-level. Suppose you hold this hand:

♠ A K J 9 7 3   ♥ K 5   ♦ Q 3   ♣ A J 4

You	**Partner**
1♠	3♦
?	

Facing 10-12 points, a slam is eminently possible. You rebid 4♣, a control-showing cuebid. This passes this message: 'A slam may be possible and I have first-round club control. What do you think of our slam prospects, partner?' If your partner doesn't like the idea of a slam he can sign off in 4♠. With a more promising hand he can make a further cuebid himself, showing a control in one of the red suits.

What does a single raise show?

So far we have discussed only hands with four-card support. What if you have three-card support? When you hold around 6-10 points, you should raise to the two-level.

Suppose partner opens 1♠ and you hold this hand:

♠ Q 9 2   ♥ 10 3   ♦ A 10 9 2   ♣ K 8 6 3

BY THE WAY

*One common method after a single raise involves Help-suit Game Tries,
which were described in* 25 Bridge
Conventions You Should Know.

You raise to 2♠. Note that the response is again in accordance with bidding to the level dictated by the total number of trumps held. You hold three trumps and you expect partner to hold five. That is a total of eight, so you bid to the eight-trick level (the two-level). When partner holds six trumps he should be willing to compete to the three-level, even when he is minimum in terms of high card points.

However many trumps partner holds, he is of course entitled to make a game try (for example, by bidding a new suit) or to raise to game. He will do this whenever his overall strength justifies such an action.

What if you hold five-card support?

A direct raise to game in partner's major shows a hand with at least five-card trump support but not much in the way of high-card points. Suppose partner opens 1♥, the next player passes and you hold:

♠ 8 6   ♥ A J 9 6 3   ♦ Q 10 7 3   ♣ 8 4

You should raise preemptively to 4♥. Partner may make the contract, he may not. What you do know is that your side has a heart fit of at least ten cards and should therefore be prepared to compete to the ten-trick level. Since your opponents are both relatively short in hearts, they will have a good fit in one of the other suits, perhaps in spades. You must make it as difficult as possible for them to locate this fit.

If your hand were any stronger, you would make a different response (as we shall see in the next section). Remember that a raise of 1♥ to 4♥ (or 1♠ to 4♠) shows a fairly weak hand with good trump support. You should not hold more than 9 HCP.

What if you are too strong for a 3♦ response?

With enough for game and four-card or longer support, you may respond with an artificial Jacoby 2NT or (with the right hand) a splinter bid. These conventions are described in *25 Bridge Conventions You Should Know*.

Suppose partner again opens 1♥, and you find yourself staring at:

♠ A 10 2   ♥ A Q 9 3   ♦ 7 2   ♣ K J 7 4

It would be entirely inappropriate to respond 4♥ on a hand of this quality. With no conventional call available, you would have to respond 2♣ in an attempt to find out more about partner's hand. Playing the Jacoby 2NT convention, you would respond 2NT. There are many different systems of rebids for the opener. In the standard version of Jacoby 2NT, for example, opener may show a short suit (singleton or void) at the three-level or a five-card suit at the four-level.

What if you are strong with three-card support?

We have already seen that on hands with three-card support and 6-10 points you give a single raise (such as 1♠ - 2♠).

With 11 points or more, and three-card support, you should respond in a different suit, intending to raise partner's suit on the next round.

♠ K 8 2   ♥ A 3   ♦ 10 9 7 4   ♣ A 10 8 5

Partner	You
1♠	2♣
2♥	2♠

Your rebid of 2♠ shows about 11-12 points and three-card spade support. It is a (non-forcing) limited bid and partner will pass unless he has some extras. It will help his final decision to know that you have only three-card support.

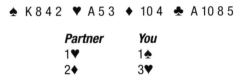

Note that you do not need to jump to 3♠, since your initial 2♣ response has already guaranteed 10+ points. In fact, the jump to 3♠ would be game-forcing, and indicate slam interest (with no slam interest, simply raise partner to 4♠ at your second turn). However, if your initial response was at the one-level, you do have to jump:

♠ K 8 4 2 ♥ A 5 3 ♦ 10 4 ♣ A 10 8 5

Partner	You
1♥	1♠
2♦	3♥

A simple 2♥ bid would show no more than 9 points and you might not even have three hearts. The jump in this auction is invitational, and indicates that you have more than your first 1♠ response promised.

Do Bergen Raises apply over a double?

When the next player makes a takeout double of partner's opening of 1♥ or 1♠, many players retain the meaning of the Bergen 3♣ and 3♦ raises. The meaning of a single raise and of a double raise remain the same too.

If you would like to make some different use of 3♣ and 3♦ (perhaps to use them as fit-showing jumps, as described in Chapter 14), you can use this alternative scheme:

LHO	Partner	RHO	You
	1♥	dbl	?

2♥	three-card or four-card raise, 6-9 points
2NT	four-card raise, 10+ points (known as Jordan or Dormer)
3♥	four-card raise, 2-6 points
redbl	choose this with 10+ HCP and three-card support.

A disadvantage of bidding this way over a double is that you do not go immediately to the three-level on hands with 6-9 points and four-card trump support. You make life much easier for the doubler's partner.

Do Bergen Raises apply over an overcall?

It is not practical to play Bergen Raises after an overcall.

LHO	Partner	RHO	You
	1♠	2♥	?

In this kind of auction, you need the bids of 3♣ and 3♦ to be natural. The best idea is to revert to this simple scheme:

2♠	three-card or four-card raise, 6-9 points
cuebid (3♥ here)	three-card or four-card raise, 10+ points
3♠	four-card raise, 2-5 points.

Unfortunately, once the opponents get into the auction, we lose the ability to distinguish easily between three-card and four-card support.

✓ Playing Bergen Raises, a response of 3♣ to one of a major shows a four-card raise based on a hand of 7-9 points. A response of 3♦ shows a four-card raise and about 10-12 points. With a hand strong enough to force to game you should use Jacoby 2NT, or make a splinter bid when you have four-card support and a side-suit singleton.

✓ A double raise of a major-suit opening (such as 1♠-3♠) is pre-emptive. It shows four-card support and 2-6 points. A single raise (1♠-2♠) shows three-card support and 6-10 points.

✓ You can choose to use Bergen Raises over an opponent's takeout double. Raises of partner's suit to the two-level and three-level also retain their meaning.

✓ When an opponent has overcalled, the 3♣ and 3♦ bids revert to their natural meaning. A cuebid shows support and 10+ points. The jump raise is still preemptive.

BERGEN RAISES

NOW TRY THESE...

1 Playing Bergen Raises, what would you respond to partner's opening of 1♠ on each of these hands?

a ♠ A 9 6 3
   ♥ Q 7 2
   ♦ 0 5
   ♣ Q 10 7 3

b ♠ A J 9 8 2
   ♥ J 6 4 3
   ♦ 8 3
   ♣ 9 5

c ♠ A Q 10 2
   ♥ K 9 6 5
   ♦ Q 7 3 2
   ♣ 3

d ♠ K J 7
   ♥ J 9 3
   ♦ A Q 10 7
   ♣ 10 9 4

e ♠ Q J 8 3
   ♥ 6 5
   ♦ Q 9 2
   ♣ A Q 8 3

f ♠ K 10 8 4
   ♥ 3
   ♦ 10 9 8 7 2
   ♣ 9 4 3

g ♠ J 8 3
   ♥ 9 6 5
   ♦ K J 9 2
   ♣ Q 8 3

h ♠ J 8 4
   ♥ Q 9 2
   ♦ A 5 4
   ♣ A K 7 2

2 Playing Bergen Raises, you open 1♠ on the following hands. What will you rebid if partner responds (i) 3♣ (ii) 3♦ (iii) 3♠?

a ♠ A K 10 7 2
   ♥ 7 3
   ♦ K 2
   ♣ A 6 4 3

b ♠ K Q J 9 6 2
   ♥ A 8 6
   ♦ 4
   ♣ A K 9

3 Playing Bergen Raises, you open 1♥ on the following hands. What will you rebid if partner responds (i) 3♣ (ii) 3♦ (iii) 3♥?

a ♠ K 8
   ♥ A K J 6 2
   ♦ Q 9 3 2
   ♣ K 7

b ♠ 8 2
   ♥ A K 10 7 5 3
   ♦ 8
   ♣ K Q J 3

ANSWERS

1 **a** 3♣   You have four spades and are within the 7-9 point range for a Bergen 3♣ response. (Playing standard responses, you would bid just 2♠.)

    b 4♠   With five-card support make the preemptive response of 4♠. The next player, who is likely to hold an excellent hand, will not enjoy this at all!

    c 4♣   You are too strong for a Bergen 3♦ raise, which should not be made when you have the playing strength for the four-level. Instead you should make a splinter bid of 4♣, showing a hand worth a raise to game and at most one club.

    d 2♦   With 11 HCP and three-card support you should start with 2♦, intending to support spades on the next round. (If you play a two-over-one system, respond with a forcing 1NT instead.)

    e 3♦   You are worth a Bergen response of 3♦. If partner rebids only 3♠, you will pass. You have already described your hand.

    f 3♠   You should bid a preemptive 3♠, showing four-card support and 2-5 points.

    g 2♠   This response shows 6-10 points and three-card support. Perfect!

    h 2♣   Respond 2♣ to find out more about partner's hand. You will probably just raise to 4♠ at your next turn.

2 **a**   If partner responds 3♣ you should sign off in 3♠. Opposite a 3♦ response you are worth 4♠. If partner makes the preemptive response of 3♠ you will pass, of course.

    b   You should bid 4♠ opposite 3♣ or 3♠. Opposite a 3♦ response a slam is possible and you should announce this with a cuebid of 4♣.

3 **a**   Bid 4♥ opposite 3♦. Opposite a 3♣ response, allow partner to make the final decision by making the in-between bid of 3♦. Opposite a preemptive raise to 3♥ you should pass.

    b   Bid 4♥ opposite all three responses. You will probably go down facing the preemptive raise but the opponents are favorites to have a game their way and (even though they have both passed at their first turn) you must ensure that they are kept quiet.

C H A P T E R

RESPONDING TO THREE-BIDS

WHAT'S IN A NAME?

The idea of preempting on weak hands goes back to auction bridge. *Milton Work* wrote, in 1926: 'To gather fully the benefits of the preempt, the bidder must have nerve. A preemptive bid is apt to fail if the bidder is timid and attempts to get off too cheaply.'

It strikes us as strange that some partnerships play a bundle of obscure conventions, ones that hardly ever arise, and yet fail to discuss much more common situations. For example, do you know how to respond to an opening preemptive three-bid? It's not the sort of thing that players tend to talk about but it is an important area of bidding and arises quite frequently.

Can you bid your own suit at the three-level?

It is clear that you should not bid a new suit, opposite partner's three-opening, unless you see some prospect of game. With a weaker hand you simply pass. A response in a new suit at the three-level should therefore be natural and forcing. It will nearly always show at least five cards in the suit that you have bid. What strength is required? To some extent it depends on the vulnerability. When partner has made a vulnerable preempt you are entitled to expect a better hand than when he is not vulnerable. Imagine this is your hand, as responder:

♠ J 4 2　♥ A K J 8 4　♦ K Q 7　♣ K 2

If partner opens a vulnerable 3♣, there is a fair chance that the club suit will run. You respond 3♥, hoping that partner can raise. If instead he rebids 3♠, showing a stopper in spades, you will try your luck in 3NT. The least helpful rebid will be 4♣, which you should pass. A club game is possible, but unlikely.

Now suppose that partner is not vulnerable when he opens 3♣. Many players would still respond 3♥ but it's usually right to pass. Preempts often force the opponents to guess — that's the whole point of them. When it's you who has a good hand, you may have to guess too!

What if partner opens 3♣ and you respond 3♦? It is unlikely that you seriously want to play in diamonds. You are probably hoping that partner can show you a stopper in a major suit, one that you do not hold strongly yourself.

Suppose partner opens 3♣ and the next player passes. You hold this hand:

♠ A K 4　♥ J 9 2　♦ K J 8 3　♣ A 7 4

You respond 3♦. If partner can rebid 3♥ you intend to play in 3NT. Otherwise you will hope for the best in 4♣.

Now look at affairs from the opener's point of view. When should he raise responder's major suit, after a sequence such as 3♣ - 3♥? It is obvious to raise with three-card support. He should also support with a doubleton honor.

Partner	You
♠ 9 2	♠ J 8 4
♥ Q 5	♥ A K J 9 3
♦ 10 4	♦ K Q 3
♣ A Q 10 9 7 3 2	♣ K 4
3♣	3♥
4♥	pass

As you see, a good 5-2 fit may be the right spot when one of the other suits is insufficiently protected for 3NT to be a sound contract.

Can you make a slam try?

What does responder have in mind on a sequence that starts 3♠ - 4♣? Is it conceivable that he would want to suggest clubs as a trump suit when he already knows that you hold seven spades? This is so unlikely that most partnerships do not use 4♣ and 4♦ responses as natural bids. Instead, they are control-showing cuebids that suggest a slam in partner's suit.

♠ A 4 2　♥ A K Q 4　♦ Q 9 7　♣ A Q 2

Over partner's 3♠, you respond 4♣. This suggests a spade slam and shows the ace or king of clubs (occasionally a singleton or void). You hope that partner holds a diamond control, so that a slam will be possible. If you are lucky enough to hear a 4♦ rebid, you will bid 4NT, Roman Keycard Blackwood. This will allow you to avoid a slam when partner has the ♦K and a queen-high trump suit.

What about a 4♥ or 4♠ response?

When partner responds 4♥ over a 3♠ opening, or jumps to 4♠ over a 3♥ opening, it is natural (and to play) rather than a cuebid. That's fairly obvious, when you think about it. A cuebid of 4♥ would deny any control in the minors and responder could not possibly be strong enough to suggest a slam in that case. Similarly a jump to 4♥ or 4♠ opposite three of a minor is natural and to play.

When is it right to bid 3NT?

A common mistake made by inexperienced players is to respond 3NT to a major-suit preempt, instead of raising partner's suit. This is a typical situation:

Partner	You
♠ K Q 10 9 7 6 3	♠ 5
♥ 8	♥ A K J 5
♦ 10 8 4	♦ A K 7 3
♣ 6 3	♣ A J 8 4
3♠	3NT!!
pass	

With secure stoppers everywhere, you might think that a notrump game will play well. Let's say you are lucky and get a heart lead, giving you three heart tricks. You may still go three down! You will be unable to reach partner's spades in notrump. You should have reasoned: 'I have five top tricks outside spades. In 4♠, partner will surely score five trumps and that will bring the total to ten.'

Notice that opener, who has already described his hand by opening 3♠, should not bid again over a 3NT response. A trustworthy partner means it when he bids 3NT. He will have a hand like this:

♠ 2   ♥ A K   ♦ Q J 7   ♣ A K Q 10 8 3 2

If the opener removes 3NT to 4♠, he will (deservedly) be in the wrong contract.

What about raising partner's suit?

What sort of hand will you have when you raise partner's preempt? Two sorts of hand are possible.

♠ A 4 2   ♥ A J 6 2   ♦ A K 7 3   ♣ 9 2

Here you would raise 3♠ to 4♠, expecting to make it. If partner has as little as seven spades to the king, you are likely to have ten tricks on top. You would raise 3♠ to game on the next hand too, but for a completely different reason.

♠ Q J 4 2　♥ 6 2　♦ K Q 7 3　♣ J 9 2

When partner opens 3♠, you know two things. First, you are likely to score seven or eight tricks in a spade contract. Second, if the opponents play the hand they will make around eleven tricks in hearts or clubs. (Your partner will have little defense for his preempt and you have nothing much to add to it.) To make it difficult for them to find such a contract, you raise the barrier to 4♠. When their strength is divided, you may even escape a double. They may suspect that you are stronger, or that you hold more shape and will be able to ruff away their aces and kings.

How does partner know if you are raising because of strength or weakness? He doesn't – but he also doesn't need to know! He has already described his own hand with the opening preempt, and should play no further part in the auction.

In the same way, you should attempt to raise partner's minor whenever you have a semblance of a fit.

♠ J 4 2　♥ 6 2　♦ K Q 7 3 2　♣ J 9 2

LHO	Partner	RHO	You
	3♣	pass	?

This is a routine raise to 4♣ at any vulnerability – the Law of Total Tricks is on your side! With one more trump, raise to 5♣.

Summary

✓ A three-level new-suit response to a preempt (such as 3♣ - 3♥) is natural and forcing.

✓ A four-level response in a minor (such as 3♥ - 4♦) is a cuebid. It shows a control in the suit bid and suggests a slam in opener's suit.

✓ The preemptor should raise partner's major-suit response (after a start such as 3♦ - 3♠) on any three cards or a doubleton honor.

✓ You can raise a preempt in two situations: when you are strong and hope to make game, or when you are weak and hope to make life difficult for the opponents.

RESPONDING TO THREE-BIDS

NOW TRY THESE...

1 Partner opens a non-vulnerable 3♣ and the next player passes. How will you respond on each of these hands?

   a   ♠ A K Q 10 7 6 3   **b**   ♠ A 4
         ♥ 7   ♥ J 6 5 4
         ♦ K Q   ♦ K 7 5 2
         ♣ J 4 3   ♣ Q 3 2

   c   ♠ Q 4   **d**   ♠ 8
         ♥ A K 10   ♥ A K J 9 6 3
         ♦ A Q J 9 7 2   ♦ A Q 7
         ♣ K 3   ♣ Q 6 3

2 Partner opens a vulnerable 3♠ and the next player passes. What will you bid on each of these hands?

   a   ♠ K J 10 5   **b**   ♠ A 10 9 6 3
         ♥ J 8 7   ♥ A K
         ♦ A K 3   ♦ A Q 10 7 4
         ♣ A 9 6   ♣ A

   c   ♠ Q 5 2   **d**   ♠ J 5
         ♥ K 8 3   ♥ A K 7 2
         ♦ 2   ♦ A K Q J 9
         ♣ Q J 10 7 6 3   ♣ A 3

3 On each of the following hands you open a non-vulnerable 3♠ and partner responds 4♣. What will you bid next?

   a   ♠ K J 9 7 6 3 2   **b**   ♠ A Q 10 8 6 3 2
         ♥ 9 4   ♥ 7
         ♦ K 9 3   ♦ 10 6
         ♣ 6   ♣ Q J 3

   c   ♠ Q 10 9 7 5 3 2   **d**   ♠ A K 9 8 7 5 2
         ♥ J 7   ♥ 7 2
         ♦ 10   ♦ 10 7
         ♣ Q 7 2   ♣ Q 4

ANSWERS

1 **a** 4♠   You know you want to play in 4♠ and there is no point at all in responding 3♠, even though it is forcing. You have relatively little defense and want to shut out the opponents.

   b 4♣   Make life hard for them by raising the level of the auction – you have little defense against 4♠. At favorable vulnerability, 5♣ might be the macho choice; the Law is not on your side, but it may be hard for the opponents to figure that out.

   c 3♦   If partner rebids 3♠ to show a spade stopper you will attempt 3NT, which will not necessarily rely on bringing in the club suit. Otherwise you will stop in 4♣.

   d 3♥   You can seek heart support, intending to play in clubs if no heart fit comes to light.

2 **a** 4♠   Chances of a slam are almost negligible. You can see seven trump tricks plus three minor-suit winners. If partner held two more tricks, he would have opened 1♠ instead of 3♠. You should raise to 4♠, rather than make a pointless cuebid.

   b 4♣   If partner can cuebid in diamonds, the grand slam will be a certainty! Otherwise you will play in 6♠, not wanting to bid a grand on a finesse.

   c 4♠   Bid game in spades, hoping to keep the other side quiet. Even if you are doubled and go down two, this will be a worthwhile sacrifice. The opponents could have made game or even slam.

   d 4NT   Bid Roman Keycard to see what trump honors partner has. If he has the ace, king and queen, you will bid 7NT. If he shows the ace and king only, bid 6♠. If he shows just the ace or king, continue with 5♦ to ask about the trump queen.

3 **a** 4♦   Partner's 4♣ was a cuebid, suggesting a slam. Since you hold reasonable trumps and a side-suit king, you should show your diamond control. This may be exactly what partner needs.

   b 4♥   With such excellent trumps and a possibly useful club holding, cuebid your singleton heart. It is not compulsory to cuebid a singleton and you would not do so on a weak hand.

   c 4♠   You are extremely weak this time and exercise your right not to cuebid a singleton.

   d 4♠   Good trumps, yes, but you have no control to cuebid. If your trump honors are all partner needs for a slam, he will bid again.

FOUR-SUIT TRANSFERS

WHAT'S IN A NAME?

Transfer bids showing a major suit opposite a 1NT opening were introduced in the 1950s. Although they were suggested by more than one person, it was **Oswald Jacoby** whose name became attached to the convention. Transfers were not extended to cover the minor suits until the 1980s.

A previous book in this series, *25 Bridge Conventions You Should Know*, described basic Jacoby transfer responses to 1NT, used to show a five-card or longer major suit. In this chapter we enhance the method so that you can also show a minor suit via a transfer. Let's begin with a brief refresher on major-suit transfers.

Major-suit transfers

When partner opens 1NT you may respond:

> 2♦   to show at least five hearts

> 2♥   to show at least five spades.

Unless opener has exceptional support (at least four cards) for the suit you have indicated, he will rebid two of your suit. What is the point of such a method? It gives you two great advantages. The first is that you will have a second chance to describe your hand, after the opener's rebid. You can continue with an invitational bid in notrump, for example, or a bid in another suit (which is forcing to game). The second benefit is that the 1NT opener will play the contract. His tenaces will be protected from the opening lead and his honor cards will be hidden from the defenders' view.

Suppose partner opens a 15-17 point 1NT and you hold this hand:

♠ 9 2 ♥ K J 6 5 3 ♦ Q 8 3 ♣ Q 10 7

Holding 8 HCP, you are too good to sign off but not quite strong enough to insist on game. You want to invite a game — you would also like to tell partner that you hold five hearts, in case there is a fit in that suit. This task is easily performed with a transfer:

Partner	You
1NT	2♦
2♥	2NT

First you show five hearts, by responding with a Jacoby transfer bid of 2♦. Next you bid 2NT to invite game. Opener now has various options. With a minimum hand he can pass 2NT, or bid 3♥ if he has at least three-card support. With a better hand he can bid either 3NT or 4♥.

Great, isn't it? Playing transfers gives you two new ways of bidding 2NT. You can make a transfer bid of either 2♦ or 2♥ on the way, thereby giving partner more information about your hand.

For players who don't play transfers, such a responding hand can be awkward to handle. A 2♥ response would be non-forcing and 3♥ would be game-forcing. You could give an indication of your values with a 2NT response but this would not show the hearts. Without transfers, it is necessary to make sure that your Stayman sequences can deal with this situation, which may create problems on other types of hands.

The 'you get another bid' advantage works well on hands of this type:

♠ Q 4 ♥ A Q 10 7 3 ♦ 9 4 ♣ A K 10 3

Partner	You
1NT	2♦
2♥	3♣

The bidding has reached only 3♣ but already you have told partner that you have five hearts, at least four clubs, and the values to play in game. If you did not play transfers you might have to start with a bid of 3♥. You would be higher already and the club suit would not yet have been shown.

We're agreed then. Transfer responses are a good thing. Since you can't have too much of a good thing in bridge, let's see how you can extend the use of transfers to show responding hands that are based on a minor suit.

What are minor-suit transfers?

Minor-suit transfers fit neatly on top of the two major-suit transfers you already know about. When partner opens 1NT, you may respond:

  2♠   to show at least six clubs

  2NT   to show at least six diamonds

    There is a question in your mind, we realize. Why does a minor-suit transfer show six cards, rather than five? The first reason is that when you are weak and want to play in 3♣ or 3♦ you will need six cards in your suit to make this a better contract than 1NT.

    Secondly, even when you are strong enough to bid game, or try for game, there is little point in showing a five-card minor when your shape is something like 3-2-3-5 – you're going to play in notrump anyway. If you have a more shapely hand with a five-card minor and a four-card major, you can start with Stayman:

BY THE WAY

Since 1NT - 2NT now shows diamonds, responder must bid a Stayman 2♣ first and then rebid 2NT to invite a notrump game (even though he has no four-card major). A sequence such as 1NT-2♣; 2♥-2NT therefore no longer guarantees that responder holds a four-card spade suit.

  ♠ A 9   ♥ Q J 6 3   ♦ 8 5   ♣ A J 10 6 3

Partner	You
1NT (15-17)	2♣
2♠	3♣

    You respond 2♣, Stayman. If partner shows four hearts, you have found a 4-4 fit in a major. Great! If instead he responds 2♦ or 2♠, you continue with 3♣. This is natural, showing five clubs, and is forcing to game. To show five clubs when your shape is 2-2-4-5 (with four diamonds), you can again start with Stayman, intending to rebid 3♣. We will look at continuations after Stayman in Chapter 9.

    So, that's why you only need to use minor-suit transfers when you hold at least six cards in the suit. In the next few sections we will see various uses for a minor-suit transfer.

What does opener do over the transfer?

You may have noticed that the minor-suit transfer bid is two levels below the next bid in the indicated suit (2♠, for example, is two bids below 3♣). Opener therefore has two possible rebids that do not go past the safety level of 3♣. With a good fit for the responder's suit (at least K-x-x), he 'breaks the transfer' by making the

BY THE WAY

When partner indicates a suit with a transfer and you reply with a minimum bid in his suit, this is known as 'accepting the transfer'. If you have a particularly good fit for his suit and show this by making some other bid, this is known as 'breaking the transfer'.

FOUR-SUIT TRANSFERS

in-between bid (2NT over 2♠ and 3♣ over 2NT). On all other hands he will 'accept (or complete) the transfer' and bid three of partner's suit. By 'breaking the transfer' with a fit, you will allow the partnership to bid 3NT sometimes with relatively few points, since the six-card minor is known to be worth six tricks.

What if you just want to sign off in a minor?

One of the most common purposes for a minor-suit transfer response is to sign off in a long suit:

Partner	You
♠ A Q J 4	♠ 10 6 2
♥ A J 8 6	♥ 4
♦ K 10 2	♦ J 9 4
♣ J 4	♣ Q 10 9 7 6 3
1NT	2♠
3♣	pass

Deciding that 3♣ will play better than 1NT, you respond 2♠ to show your six-card club suit. Partner has no special support for clubs, so he accepts the transfer. He rebids 3♣ and you pass. Even if partner had rebid 2NT instead, showing good support for clubs, you would have had no interest in game on this particular hand. You would have signed off in 3♣ yourself.

The bidding would have gone similarly if you had been dealt a weak hand with a six-card diamond suit. You would have started with 2NT, intending to play in 3♦.

How do you invite 3NT?

When you hold game-try values and a minor suit that may yield six tricks if partner has a good fit, you again start with a transfer.

Partner	You
♠ A J 4	♠ 10 6
♥ A 10 8 6	♥ 7 4
♦ K 10 2	♦ Q 9 4
♣ A 10 4	♣ K Q 9 7 6 3
1NT	2♠
2NT	3NT
pass	

You can see a good chance of 3NT if partner has A-x-x in the club suit. You respond with 2♠ and partner shows a good fit by bidding 2NT instead of 3♣.

Even though there is no guarantee of three quick tricks outside, you bid 3NT here and will surely be rewarded with a game bonus on this particular occasion. If instead partner had denied good support, you would have passed the 3♣ rebid.

BY THE WAY

The 1NT opener may use his judgment in deciding whether to make the in-between bid. Suppose he holds K-x-x in partner's minor but has a bundle of queens and jacks in the other suits and only one ace. The chance of three outside quick tricks is reduced and he may choose not to show a good fit.

Can you still show a second suit?

What happens when partner opens 1NT and you hold game or slam values and 6-4 shape including a six-card minor and four cards in a higher suit? You show the minor with a transfer response and then bid your four-card suit at the three-level.

♠ J   ♥ A Q 7 2   ♦ 10 5   ♣ K Q 10 7 6 2

Partner opens 1NT and you respond 2♠, showing long clubs. Whether or not partner breaks the transfer, you will continue with 3♥ to show that you have 6-4 shape. As always when you bid a second suit after a transfer, this sequence is game-forcing. Partner can now show support for either suit or bid 3NT to deny a fit anywhere. (Remember that with a five-card minor and a four-card major suit, you would have started with Stayman instead.)

What if you have a minor two-suiter?

At the start of this chapter we said that a minor-suit transfer showed at least a six-card suit. Even writers of respectable bridge books sometimes tell a small lie. There is one situation in which you use a minor-suit transfer on a five-card suit — when you have a powerful minor two-suiter. Here is an example:

Partner	You
♠ A Q 4	♠ 10 5
♥ K J 6	♥ A
♦ J 8 3 2	♦ A Q 10 6 4
♣ A J 6	♣ K Q 9 5 2
1NT	2NT
3♦	4♣
4♦	4♥
4♠	4NT
5♥	6♦

You respond 2NT to show your diamonds and then rebid 4♣, a sequence that shows at least 5-5 in the minor suits. (If you happemed to have longer clubs than diamonds, it would be correct to transfer to clubs first.) Partner's 4♦ sets the trump suit and you continue with 4♥, a control-showing cuebid that invites a slam. Partner co-operates by cuebidding his spade control and you use Roman Keycard Blackwood. The response shows two keycards (the black aces on this occasion) and an excellent slam is reached.

What if you have a strong hand with just one suit?

Suppose you have only one suit, which is at least six cards long, and you can see a chance for slam when partner opens 1NT. What then? Whether the suit is a major or a minor, you do not use a transfer response. Instead you jump to three of your suit.

♠ K 10 3   ♥ Q 2   ♦ A Q J 8 7 3   ♣ A 6

You respond 3♦ to 1NT and partner must now judge if his hand is suitable for a diamond slam.

These will be positive indicators for the 1NT bidder:

A fit for diamonds

Nearer 17 HCP than 15

Good controls (aces and kings)

These will be negative indicators for the 1NT bidder:

Poor fit for diamonds

Nearer 15 HCP than 17

Several queens and jacks, rather than aces and kings.

Bearing these factors in mind, opener will either sign off in 3NT or cuebid a control in a new suit.

When responder has indicated a six-card major suit and slam interest (1NT - 3♥, or 1NT - 3♠), opener should sign off in four of the major only when he has a relatively poor hand with worse than Q-x in the trump suit. With other minimum hands he should cuebid his cheapest control, not intending to carry the bidding past the game level. Suppose you hold these cards:

♠ Q 7   ♥ Q J 8 2   ♦ K 3 2   ♣ A Q J 5

You	Partner
1NT	3♠
?	

You have only two trumps, 15 HCP and too many queens and jacks to rate your hand highly for slam purposes. Nevertheless, bid 4♣ to show the ♣A. If partner continues with 4♦ or 4♥, you will sign off in 4♠. This indicates that your hand is not especially strong and you are leaving any further slam move to him.

As the chapters of this book tick by, you will see more and more references to control-showing cuebids. That's the way modern slam bidding works, particularly when strong players are at the table. If you cannot wait to hear more about this style of bidding, feel free to leap ahead to Chapter 20!

✓ A transfer into a major (2♦ for hearts, 2♥ for spades) shows at least a five-card suit. A transfer into a minor (2♠ for clubs, 2NT for diamonds) usually shows a six-card or longer suit.

✓ With at least K-x-x in partner's minor, the opener will usually 'break the transfer', bidding 2NT over 2♠ (or 3♣ over 2NT). This will allow responder to detect low point-count 3NT contracts based on six running tricks in the minor.

✓ With a five-card minor and a four-card major suit and a game-forcing hand, responder should start with Stayman. If no major-suit fit comes to light, he can then bid his five-card minor at the three-level.

✓ With a six-card minor and four cards in a higher suit and a game-forcing hand, responder transfers into the minor and then shows his second suit at the three-level.

✓ With a strong hand that is at least 5-5 in the minors, responder starts with a 2NT response (showing the diamonds) and then rebids 4♣. With longer clubs (at least 6-5 shape), transfer into clubs first.

✓ With potential slam values and just one suit, at least six cards in length, responder should jump to the three-level in his suit rather than using a transfer.

FOUR-SUIT TRANSFERS

NOW TRY THESE...

1 On each of these hands partner opens 1NT, showing 15-17 HCP. What do you respond, playing four-suit transfers, and what will you bid next?

a
♠ J 3
♥ J 4
♦ A 10 9 8 7 3
♣ 9 8 5

b
♠ 9 7 4
♥ A 6
♦ 5 3
♣ K 10 9 7 6 3

c
♠ A J 6 2
♥ 7
♦ A K J 7 4
♣ 8 5 3

d
♠ 7 2
♥ Q 8
♦ J 10 6 2
♣ A Q 10 7 6

e
♠ 10 6
♥ J 9 2
♦ 8 3
♣ A Q J 8 5 3

f
♠ 9
♥ K Q 7 2
♦ A K J 7 6 2
♣ K 2

g
♠ K 6 5
♥ 10
♦ A K 10 8 6 3
♣ A J 2

h
♠ A Q 3
♥ K Q J 9 7 6
♦ 4
♣ K 10 2

2 Here you open 1NT and partner responds 2♠. What do you rebid?

a
♠ K 9 2
♥ K 10 8 4
♦ A Q 4
♣ A 10 4

b
♠ K Q 10 3
♥ Q 9 6
♦ K Q 4
♣ K 8 7

3 Here you open 1NT and partner responds 3♣. What do you rebid?

a
♠ K 5
♥ Q 10 8 2
♦ A Q 7 6
♣ A 9 7

b
♠ Q J 5 4
♥ K Q 10 7
♦ K Q 4
♣ Q 6

ANSWERS

1 **a** **2NT** Whether or not partner breaks the transfer (by making the in-between bid of 3♣), you intend to play in 3♦.

    b **2♠** If partner shows a good fit for your club suit, by bidding 2NT, you will rebid 3NT. Otherwise you will play in 3♣. Either way, you may not be in the right contract. You will have a better chance, though, thanks to minor-suit transfers!

    c **2♣** With only five diamonds, you first seek a spade fit by bidding Stayman. If partner responds 2♦ or 2♥, you will rebid 3♦ to show five diamonds. This sequence is forcing to game.

    d **3NT** With more points, and therefore some slam possibilities, you could seek support for the clubs by starting with Stayman and rebidding 3♣. Here even eleven tricks is too ambitious a goal, and you should respond 3NT.

    e **3NT** Even if partner does not hold the club king, it is likely that you will have a reasonable chance of making 3NT. In particular he may hold ♣K-x and not be in a position to break a 2♠ transfer.

    f **2NT** With 6-4 shape, you show the minor first via a transfer. You plan to rebid 3♥.

    g **3♦** A slam is possible and you have a single six-card suit. You therefore bid the suit at the three-level. Partner might rebid 3NT to deny slam interest. On better hands, he will cuebid his cheapest control.

    h **3♥** Exactly the same method is used when you have a six-card major. Partner will cuebid unless he has a poor hand for slam purposes. In that case he can sign off in 4♥.

2 **a** **2NT** With A-x-x in clubs and fine prospects of quick tricks outside, you are happy to make the in-between bid. Partner may now
    be   able to bid a low point-count 3NT.

    b **3♣** Here prospects are not so good. You have Q-x-x in partner's suit, yes, but not a single ace outside. Even if the clubs are good for six tricks, a low point-count 3NT may well go down.

3 **a** **3♦** Only 15 HCP, yes, but you have fine support for partner's six-card club suit and good controls (aces and kings) outside. You cuebid your cheapest control.

    b **3NT** With 15 HCP, poor support and few controls, you sign off.

GAMBLING 3NT

WHAT'S IN A NAME?

 The Gambling 3NT opening was part of the original Acol system, devised in the late 1930s at the Acol Road Bridge Club in North London. Still widely played around the world, particularly in Britain, Acol was created by five big names of that era: **Jack Marx**, **Maurice Harrison-Gray**, **S. J. Simon**, **Terence Reese** and **Iain Macleod**.

In the early days of bridge, an opening bid of 3NT showed a very strong balanced hand, with somewhere in the region of 25-27 HCP. However, it is not attractive to open a strong hand at such a high level, since doing so leaves very little space for partner to bid constructively. Openings at the three-level and four-level are usually reserved for weak hands with a long suit. You use such openings to remove bidding space from the opponents, not from yourselves! So, nowadays, it is normal to open 2♣ on very strong balanced hands, intending to rebid in notrump. You can therefore use a 3NT opening for a different purpose.

The most common use for this opening is to show a solid seven-card minor, with no card higher than a queen outside. This would be a typical hand for a 'Gambling 3NT' opening:

♠ 10 5 ♥ 2 ♦ Q 6 3 ♣ A K Q J 8 6 3

Partner may pass the opening bid and leave you to play in 3NT. Usually this will be because he holds sufficient stoppers in the other suits to give you a good chance of making the contract. If he has only two suits stopped, he may still judge it best to pass. Perhaps the defenders will not find the best lead.

How disciplined should you be with the 3NT opening? What if your seven-card minor is headed by the A-K-Q instead of the A-K-Q-J — should you still open 3NT? Many players would, some players wouldn't. If partner has a doubleton in the suit, A-K-Q-x-x-x-x is a near-certainty to run without loss. If he holds a singleton, you will just need a 3-2 break.

What if you have an eight-card solid suit? Some players would still open 3NT but you may have more success by bidding five of the minor. With an eight-card suit you can make one more trick playing in a suit contract your way. The need to preempt is also greater, since the opponents are very likely to hold a good fit their way. Your hand will be almost useless on defense, because the opponents can surely ruff the second (or first) round of your long suit.

It depends on your personal style whether you are willing to 'bend' conventional bids (in other words, to make them when you do not have the precise requirements). However, it is not good for partnership confidence (or your score, usually!) to stray from your agreements with any regularity. In particular, when you open 3NT in the first or second position make sure that you do not hold any card higher than a queen outside the long suit. It will become impossible for partner to make a sensible decision on whether or not to bid on if you break that rule.

Should you bid over 3NT?

Suppose partner opens with a Gambling 3NT and you hold these cards:

♠ A K 6 5   ♥ K 10 7 4   ♦ 9 7 4   ♣ 9 3

It is attractive to pass 3NT. If a spade or a heart is led, there will be a chance for nine tricks. If the opponents do manage to cash the first five or six tricks against 3NT… well, you can't win them all. Since you might go down anyway playing in four of partner's long suit, you might as well try for the game bonus in 3NT.

You would be very happy to let 3NT stand on this type of hand:

♠ A J 5 4   ♥ A 7 4 3   ♦ 10 7 4   ♣ 9 3

If partner's suit is diamonds it is quite likely that the opponents can take five club tricks. Even then, the defender on lead might hold only three clubs or might have a major suit that is longer, and lead that instead. When partner's suit is clubs, there is the additional chance that he may hold a doubleton diamond with the suit breaking 4-4. So, err towards boldness when you have to decide whether to let the 3NT opening stand or run to four of partner's suit. Always remember that it may be no picnic to score ten tricks in the minor. The opponents may also be more inclined to double that contract.

What if you don't think 3NT is the right spot?

Let's look next at a hand where you do not want partner to play in 3NT.

♠ J 7 3   ♥ K Q 6 2   ♦ 10 7 4   ♣ Q 9 3

With this hand in the dummy 3NT could prove expensive, particularly if you are vulnerable. You should respond 4♣, which means 'let's play in four of your suit'. When partner holds diamonds, he will correct to 4♦. Note that you must respond 4♣ even though you know (because you can see the ♣Q in your own hand) that partner's solid suit is diamonds. A response of 4♦ can have a different meaning, as we will see in a moment.

As responder, you have a very accurate picture of partner's hand. You can tell not only how many tricks you can make if you play the contract, but also how many tricks the opponents are likely to make in their best suit. What would you respond on this fairly weak hand?

♠ 6 5 3   ♥ Q 7 4   ♦ K Q 8 2   ♣ 9 8 3

LHO	Partner	RHO	You
	3NT	pass	?

Partner has a solid club suit and not much outside. How many tricks can your side make if clubs are trumps? Probably eight and maybe nine, if partner has three cards in diamonds. How many tricks can the opponents score in their best major-suit fit? At least ten, and maybe eleven or twelve! Not vulnerable (and even perhaps with both vulnerable) you should respond 5♣, making it difficult for the opponents to find their fit. On a good day you may survive without being doubled.

Sometimes you will be able to diagnose a high-level contract in partner's suit. What would you respond to 3NT on this hand?

♠ K 5   ♥ A K Q 7 4   ♦ A 7 4   ♣ 9 5 4

LHO	Partner	RHO	You
	3NT	pass	?

You should respond 6♣! Since you will be playing the contract, the spade suit is safe from attack. Meanwhile there is an excellent chance that you can score seven clubs, four hearts (possibly after setting up the suit with a ruff) and the ♦A. You will be declarer, so the ♠K will be protected from the opening lead.

Is there a clever slam try available?

Are you sure you really want to know about this? Well... okay. We have already seen that a 4♦ response is not necessary in a natural sense. When you want to remove partner's 3NT opening and can tell (from the honors in your own hand) that partner holds diamonds, you still respond 4♣ and let him correct to 4♦. But bridge players like to assign a meaning to every bid! The inventors of the Gambling 3NT therefore suggested that a response of 4♦ should ask opener if he holds a singleton anywhere.

These are opener's rebids after 3NT - 4♦:

LHO	Partner	RHO	You
	3NT	pass	4♦
pass	?		

4♥	singleton heart
4♠	singleton spade
4NT	no singleton (7-2-2-2 shape)
5♣	long clubs and a singleton diamond
5♦	long diamonds and a singleton club

You may think it would be easier to remember if 5♦ showed a singleton diamond. This response would carry you past the safety level of 5♣, however, on those occasions when a singleton diamond was of no help to partner.

Here's a hand (cleverly constructed by the authors), where the 4♦ inquiry will work to good advantage.

Partner	You
♠ J 10 3	♠ A 9
♥ 6	♥ Q 9 5
♦ 9 4	♦ A K Q 7 3
♣ A K Q J 8 5 3	♣ 10 6 4
3NT	4♦
4♥	6♣

You are willing to play in 5♣ anyway, so you respond 4♦, just in case partner has a singleton heart. When partner does indeed show such a feature, you leap to 6♣. Provided the diamonds break no worse than 4-2, you will be able to set up a twelfth trick in that suit. If partner had made any other response to the 4♦ inquiry (4♠, 4NT or 5♣), you would have settled for game in clubs. You would know that there were two top losers in hearts.

Summary

✓ The Gambling 3NT opening shows a solid seven-card minor suit. In first or second position you should hold no card higher than a queen outside. In third or fourth position some players are willing to make the bid with an ace or king outside.

✓ When responder wants to play at some level in opener's suit, he responds in clubs, expecting partner to correct to diamonds when that is his suit.

✓ A response of 4♦ can be used to ask opener to identify any side-suit singleton that he holds. With a major-suit singleton he bids four of that suit. With a minor-suit singleton he bids five of the other minor (his solid suit). With no singleton he bids 4NT.

GAMBLING 3NT

NOW TRY THESE...

1 Playing the Gambling 3NT, what opening bid would you make on each of these hands in the first or second seat? Would your action change in the third seat?

a ♠ 6
♥ Q 7
♦ 10 5 4
♣ A K Q J 9 7 3

b ♠ —
♥ Q J 4 3
♦ A K Q J 8 5 2
♣ 10 5

c ♠ 8
♥ Q 9 5
♦ J 2
♣ A K J 10 8 3 2

d ♠ 6
♥ J 10 3
♦ 7
♣ A K Q J 8 7 6 2

2 How would you respond to an opening bid of 3NT on each of these hands?

a ♠ J 10 7 2
♥ Q 8 5 2
♦ K Q 2
♣ 6 3

b ♠ K 2
♥ A K J 10 6 4
♦ 9 4
♣ A Q 5

c ♠ J 10 7
♥ A K Q 7 2
♦ A 2
♣ 9 7 2

d ♠ A 9 8 2
♥ A K Q 6
♦ 9 4
♣ 10 7 4

3 What will you rebid on each hand after this start to the auction?

You	Partner
3NT	4♦
?	

a ♠ Q 7
♥ J 6 2
♦ 9
♣ A K Q J 7 5 3

b ♠ 8 2
♥ Q 5
♦ A K Q J 10 6 2
♣ 9 3

ANSWERS

1 **a** 3NT Perfect in every way!

    b 1♦ The playing strength is too good for a preemptive 3NT opening, not to mention the side four-card major. You could make a slam opposite various hands where partner would attempt to sign off in 4♦!

    c 1♣ The suit is not good enough for a Gambling 3NT opening. That said, there are some players (those who like a bit of action...) who would risk a 3NT opening in third seat.

    d 5♣ Again, some players would open 3NT. However, with 8-3-1-1 shape, the playing strength is good in clubs and the defense against any contract by the opponents almost nonexistent. A 5♣ opening is a superior move in first, second or third seat.

2 **a** 4♣ You have a stopper, of sorts, in each of the side suits, but the opponents are likely to take at least seven tricks against 3NT.

    b 6♦ The odds are good that you can set up the hearts and score twelve tricks on any lead. Even though partner would correct 6♣ to 6♦, this would not be a good response. If partner plays the contract you might get a spade lead through the king.

    c 4♦ You are willing to play in 5♣. If partner holds a singleton spade, 6♣ should be a playable contract.

    d 5♣ You want to play in five of partner's minor. If partner's solid suit is diamonds, he will correct to 5♦.

3 **a** 5♣ Partner's 4♦ response asks if you hold a singleton. When the singleton is in a minor suit, you rebid five of your long suit.

    b 4NT With no singleton to show, you rebid 4NT. If partner continues with 5♣, he will still expect you to correct to 5♦.

D.O.N.T. DEFENSE TO A STRONG 1NT

WHAT'S IN A NAME?

Devised by **Marty Bergen**, D.O.N.T. is short for 'Disturb Opponent's NoTrump'. Like Bergen Raises, this convention is based on the Law of Total Tricks – if you can find an eight-card fit you are safe at the two-level, even with fewer high cards than the opponents.

What is the purpose of getting into the auction against a strong 1NT opening? The scoring table is such that a declarer in 1NT, particularly when not vulnerable, rarely ends up with a poor score. Suppose dummy holds a near-bust and declarer goes down two not vulnerable, losing 100. In a matchpoint event there will be plenty of pairs making 110 and 140 the other way. Also, 1NT is a difficult contract to defend. Declarer can see his combined assets. On defense, you and your partner may not discover your best suit until it is too late. So, when you have a bit of shape, there is every incentive to enter the bidding.

Will you go for a big number when the next hand is strong? Occasionally, yes, but some pairs use a double by the 1NT opener's partner for takeout. Even those who do use a penalty double may be scared of picking up an inadequate penalty when they can make a game their way. The odds are in your favor, especially when you are not vulnerable!

When the opponents are playing a strong 1NT, you will rarely hold a hand that justifies a penalty double. Even when you do, the opponents will usually have a playable spot in their longest combined holding. It therefore makes good sense to give the double a conventional meaning, and to include it as part of your machinery for attempting to buy the contract yourself. The D.O.N.T. convention is one that does this.

What is D.O.N.T.?

Playing D.O.N.T., when an opponent opens a strong 1NT, you may enter the auction (in either second or fourth seat) with one of these calls:

dbl	a single-suiter somewhere (2♣ asks which suit)
2♣	clubs and a higher suit
2♦	diamonds and a higher suit
2♥	hearts and spades
2♠	six-card spades (weaker hand than via a double)
2NT	the minor suits, at least 5-5 shape

How many points do you need to take one of these actions? The answer is: not many! The whole idea of the method is to dislodge your opponent from 1NT. Will he be pleased when you enter the auction? Not at all. Every good player expects at least a 65% score when declaring a 1NT contract. By entering the auction you rob him of this pleasure. So, you can enter the bidding with as little as 7 points, although you might have as much as 15. With such a wide range, you may wonder how partner can tell if you can make game your way. This is very unlikely, against a strong 1NT, and in general you should forget about such a prospect unless a good major-suit fit comes to light. The purpose of D.O.N.T. is not to find games for yourself but to disturb the opponents' 1NT contract whenever you have a bit of shape.

What shape do you need? For the 2♣/2♦/2♥ overcalls, which show two-suiters, you should be at least 5-4, but the suits can be either way round. You might bid 2♣ on a hand with five hearts and four clubs, or on a hand with four hearts and five clubs.

This a typical hand for the convention:

♠ 10 3 ♥ K J 10 7 5 2 ♦ Q 9 5 ♣ J 3

LHO	Partner	RHO	You
		1NT	?

You enter with a double, intending to play in 2♥. What if the next player is strong and you end up doubled in 2♥? There is no reason to expect a bad score, at least when you are not vulnerable. You are only at the two-level and the opponents may well have a game their way.

Suppose instead that you hold a two-suiter:

♠ A 10 9 3 ♥ 4 ♦ 8 3 2 ♣ K J 9 7 4

LHO	Partner	RHO	You
		1NT	?

Here you will bid 2♣ (clubs and a higher suit). You happen to hold five clubs, but you are not promising more than four.

You get the idea, then. You don't need much of a hand to get into the bidding. Let's look next at how the auction may continue after the various possible D.O.N.T. actions.

BY THE WAY

In the standard version of D.O.N.T. you bid 2♠ with a weak six-carder in spades and start with a double on a stronger spade six-carder. An alternative is to play that the double shows a single-suiter in clubs, diamonds or hearts. You bid 2♠ with spades. Some pairs play that double followed by 2♠ shows six spades and a four-card minor, while a direct 2♠ shows only spades.

BY THE WAY

It is possible to modify D.O.N.T. for use against a weak notrump opening, but in our view the lack of a penalty double is a serious drawback. We recommend its use only against strong notrump openings.

How do you bid over partner's D.O.N.T. double?

When partner doubles, he shows a six-card suit somewhere. If the next player passes you will generally respond 2♣, expecting partner to pass with clubs and to bid his long suit otherwise. Suppose you hold these cards:

♠ A K 10 4 ♥ K 2 ♦ J 10 9 8 2 ♣ 8 3

LHO	Partner	RHO	You
1NT	dbl	pass	?

The first point to make is that it would be a big gamble to pass. Your partner's double has shown a possibly moderate hand with a six-card suit somewhere. You might defeat 1NT, you might not. Unless you are a professional gambler or thrill seeker, you should choose to play in partner's long suit. You achieve this by responding 2♣. Because you are short in hearts and clubs, you rather expect partner to pass 2♣ or to rebid 2♥. If he surprises you by bidding 2♠, you could suggest a game by raising to 3♠.

If you have a decent six-card suit of your own, you can often bid it directly:

♠ Q J 6   ♥ A J 10 7 6 2   ♦ 8 5 2   ♣ 7

LHO	Partner	RHO	You
1NT	dbl	pass	?

Here you would bid 2♥. That's because you expect partner to pass a 2♣ response and you hope that 2♥ will be a better contract. Suppose you held the same hand with the minor suits reversed (one diamond and three clubs). You might then bid 2♣, happy to play in a 6-3 club fit if that turned out to be partner's suit. If he corrected to 2♦, showing six cards opposite your singleton, you could then bid 2♥.

Is it ever wise to pass a double? In bridge you are allowed to do almost anything! If you found yourself with a balanced 15-count, you could pass. Don't hold your breath, though, waiting for this to happen!

What if there is a bid over partner's double?

It is an admitted weakness of the D.O.N.T. defense that you do not identify your suit immediately when you double to show a one-suiter (it is similar in this regard to the Cappelletti 2♣ bid that we talked about in Chapter 1). It doesn't cost you at all when the auction is not contested further, but suppose you encounter this situation:

♠ 10 8 5 2   ♥ K J 6 4   ♦ J 3   ♣ A 8 7

LHO	Partner	RHO	You
1NT	dbl	2♠	?

If you were playing natural overcalls and your partner had overcalled 2♣ or 2♥, you would give him a raise. If his overcall had been 2♦ you would not raise. What should you do now, when partner has made a D.O.N.T. double to show a single-suiter? The best bet is to ask for partner's suit, with a double (remember from Chapter 1, this is for takeout, since partner's suit is unknown). If he does happen to have diamonds, it will not be a disaster to play in a 6-2 fit. The general rule is to be aggressive in this situation. Otherwise you will do worse than those who are playing a different method, one without this inherent competitive weakness.

How does the bidding continue after 2♣ or 2♦?

When partner overcalls 2♣, you do not know what his second suit is and will sometimes have to guess what to do. Suppose you hold these cards:

♠ Q 9 7 4   ♥ 10 8   ♦ A 9 8 6 3   ♣ 8 2

LHO	Partner	RHO	You
1NT	2♣	pass	?

BY THE WAY

Remember that your main objective is to dislodge an opponent from 1NT, not to look for a game your way. When partner enters the auction with a D.O.N.T. bid, d.o.n.t. punish him by raising too high!

Should you pass or bid 2♦, which asks for partner's second suit? If partner has four hearts and five clubs, you will do best to pass 2♣. If he has five hearts and four clubs, or if his other suit is spades or diamonds, you will do better to bid 2♦. It's a guess, and that is part of the package you accept when you play this convention. You are causing plenty of hassle for the other side and occasionally you pay for it with some inconvenience to yourself. As a general guideline, you should keep the bidding as low as possible, particularly when you are weak. Here you should pass 2♣. If you are doubled in that contract, then you can consider trying to escape.

When partner overcalls 2♦, he shows diamonds and a major. You can either pass, to play in diamonds, or respond 2♥ to ask which major he has.

♠ A 9 6 3   ♥ 10 8   ♦ J 9 6   ♣ K 10 8 2

LHO	Partner	RHO	You
1NT	2♦	pass	?

If partner has four or five spades, you would like to play in that suit. It is much more likely that he has four or five hearts, particularly as RHO did not bid hearts himself. So, you should pass 2♦, accepting that you have some kind of fit in that suit. The object of the method is to stop your opponent playing in 1NT. Don't concern yourself too much about finding your own best fit — at any rate not when the price you pay for extended searching is that you may play in a very poor fit.

Very rarely, you may have a very strong hand and think that game may be on, despite the enemy 1NT bid. What should you do? The only strong response to 2♣ or 2♦ is 2NT. Unfortunately there is not much that partner can then do to tell you how strong the overcall was. He will usually have to bid his other suit at the three-level and you will be none the wiser about his point-count. At least you will be able to detect a 4-4 major-suit fit:

Partner	You
♠ K 9 6 2	♠ A Q 10 5
♥ 7	♥ K Q 8 4 2
♦ K Q 10 6 3	♦ 9 2
♣ 9 7 2	♣ A 6

LHO	Partner	RHO	You
1NT (15-17)	2♦	pass	2NT
pass	3♣	pass	4♠
all pass			

All will be well on this occasion.

What if partner's 2♣ or 2♦ is doubled?

Quite often your partner's D.O.N.T. overcall of 2♣ or 2♦ will be doubled by the next player. There are several possible meanings of the opponent's double: a double of 2♣ might be (a) Stayman, (b) points or (c) penalties. It is a pointless strain on your memory, and entirely unproductive, to vary your action in the fourth seat according to the meaning of the opponent's double. You should pass when you want to play in the suit that partner has already bid, or redouble to ask partner to bid his second suit. (The memory-guide is 'Pass to Play, Redouble for Rescue'.) If instead you bid a new suit yourself, this will show a six-card suit.

♠ J 8 7 5   ♥ 10 8 3   ♦ A J 10 9 6   ♣ 2

LHO	Partner	RHO	You
1NT	2♣	dbl	redbl

Allowing partner to play in 2♣ doubled does not appeal, so you redouble. This asks partner to bid his other suit. Bidding 2♦ instead would show a six-card suit of your own and ask partner to pass.

If you don't like partner's other suit, you have the option of bidding a long suit of your own at that stage:

♠ Q 10 9 7 5 3   ♥ Q 10 8 3   ♦ 8 3   ♣ 2

LHO	Partner	RHO	You
1NT	2♣	dbl	redbl
pass	2♦	pass	?

Had partner rebid 2♥ (or 2♠!) you would be happy to pass. As it is, you can retreat to 2♠ now.

What if partner's 2♣ or 2♦ is overcalled?

When RHO has a five-card suit of his own he may compete over your partner's 2♣ or 2♦ overcall. A double by you at that point is for takeout, asking partner to bid his second suit.

♠ A 10 9 4   ♥ 10 8 3   ♦ K Q 7 6   ♣ 5 2

LHO	Partner	RHO	You
1NT	2♣	2♥	?

You double, asking partner for his second suit. This allows you to compete in 2♠ or 3♦, wherever your fit is. It's entirely possible that you will go one down but in that case they would probably have made 2♥. You can't afford to sell out at such a low level when the points are fairly evenly divided between the two sides.

You might also double on a hand with support for opener's minor:

♠ 9 6   ♥ A 10 8 3   ♦ K 6 3   ♣ Q 10 5 2

LHO	Partner	RHO	You
1NT	2♣	2♦	?

The bidding starts 1NT - 2♣ - 2♦. Again you would double, to ask for partner's second suit. If he rebids 2♥, you will play in hearts. If instead he rebids 2♠, you will retreat to 3♣. (Fun, isn't it?)

How does the bidding continue after 2♥ and 2♠?

When partner bids 2♥, your workload is lighter. You must simply choose one of the major suits.

♠ K J   ♥ 5 3   ♦ J 9 6 3 2   ♣ 10 8 5 4

LHO	Partner	RHO	You
1NT	2♥	pass	?

You should pass rather than bid 2♠. This may save you from a double when partner holds four spades and five hearts. If 2♥ does get doubled, you will have the option of bidding 2♠ at that point. When the situation looks ominous, be happy to play anywhere undoubled.

Opposite 2♥ the rare response of 2NT is again strong. The overcaller must attempt to describe his hand. Suppose you have:

♠ K 10 8 3   ♥ A Q 8 7 3   ♦ 6 2   ♣ 10 7

LHO	Partner	RHO	You
		1NT	2♥
pass	2NT	pass	?

Partner is interested in game. Since your hand is nothing special, you rebid 3♥ to show five cards in that suit and only four in the other major. If you were 5-5 in the majors, you would rebid 3♣ so that partner could choose trumps. With an upper-range hand, you would accept the game try and make a similar rebid at the four-level.

When partner has overcalled 2♠ (showing a weak hand with six spades), you should look for game only when you have a good spade fit.

♠ A 9 7 2   ♥ K Q 5 4   ♦ 8   ♣ K 9 7 2

LHO	Partner	RHO	You
1NT	2♠	pass	?

Here you can respond 2NT, asking partner to bid game with a maximum. If instead you bid 3♠ (perhaps over a takeout double or bid by the third player), this would be competitive, not invitational.

Summary

✓ The object of the D.O.N.T. defense is to force your opponent out of his 1NT contract. The method is obstructive and you should generally seek your best fit at the two-level, rather than wonder if you can make game somewhere.

✓ Double shows a one-suiter; 2♣ shows clubs and a higher suit; 2♦ shows diamonds and a major; 2♥ shows the majors; 2♠ shows a weak single-suiter in spades and 2NT shows the minors.

✓ In response to 2♣ or 2♦ you may make the next higher bid to ask what partner's second suit is.

✓ On the rare occasions you have a really strong hand opposite a D.O.N.T. overcall, a bid of 2NT can be used to ask for more information from partner.

D.O.N.T. DEFENSE TO A STRONG 1NT

NOW TRY THESE...

1 Playing D.O.N.T., what will you bid when RHO opens a strong 1NT?

a
♠ A 9 7 6 4
♥ 10 7 3
♦ 5
♣ A Q 8 7

b
♠ J 3
♥ K 9 3
♦ Q J 9 7 5 3
♣ 9 5

c
♠ K 9 7 5
♥ K 10 7 6 3
♦ 7 2
♣ 6 3

d
♠ 8 5
♥ 3
♦ K J 10 5 4
♣ A J 9 7 3

e
♠ Q J 9 8 2
♥ 6 3
♦ A 10 9 8 2
♣ 9

f
♠ A K 9 7 6 3
♥ 9 8 3
♦ A 8
♣ J 6

2 How will you respond to partner's D.O.N.T. 2♣?

LHO	Partner	RHO	You
1NT	2♣	pass	?

a
♠ A 5
♥ 8 7
♦ K 10 8 7 5 2
♣ 9 6 4

b
♠ Q 9 7
♥ A 10 9 6 3
♦ K 9 4
♣ 10 8

c
♠ K Q 10 9 6 4
♥ 9 3
♦ A 4
♣ 10 7 6

d
♠ 9 5
♥ K 10 8 7 2
♦ Q 9 6 2
♣ 8 3

3 How will you respond to partner's D.O.N.T. 2♦?

LHO	Partner	RHO	You
1NT	2♦	pass	?

a
♠ K Q 7 3
♥ 9 3
♦ J 9 3
♣ K 10 9 4

b
♠ K 10 8 6 2
♥ 9 7 4
♦ 10 2
♣ A K 3

c
♠ 8 6
♥ 7 4
♦ A Q 10 5 4 3
♣ 10 8 6

d
♠ A 9 4
♥ A J 8
♦ A 7 6 5 4 2
♣ 4

ANSWERS

1 **a** **2♣**   Perfect for clubs and another suit. If partner responds 2♦, you will rebid 2♠. Remember you can be 5-4 or 4-5 in your two suits.

     b **dbl**   You indicate a single-suiter with a double, thereby achieving your objective of dislodging the opponent from 1NT. Your extra nines give this weak-looking hand some solidity; even if you get doubled in 2♦, it won't be the end of the world.

     c **2♥**   If you were vulnerable, you would need to be 'courageous' or 'foolhardy' (choose your adjective) to make this bid!

     d **2NT**   With 5-5 shape and reasonable playing strength, you can bid as high as 2NT. With only 5-4 or 4-5 in the minors, you would prefer 2♣.

     e **2♦**   Diamonds and a higher suit. Easy!

     f **dbl**   A robust single-suiter in spades, so you start with a double. A 2♠ bid would show a weaker hand.

2 **a** **pass**   Remember that 2♦ would ask partner to show his other suit.

     b **2♦**   The hearts are not good enough for 2♥, so you will play in partner's second suit.

     c **2♠**   Your spades are good enough to insist on them as a trump suit. Partner does not guarantee five clubs, remember, so you are not guaranteed a good fit if you pass instead.

     d **pass**   East's failure to bid spades suggests that partner has the black suits. Keep the bidding low, particularly when you are weak and fear a double.

3 **a** **pass**   If you bid 2♠, you may switch a 5-3 fit for a 4-2 (or worse!) one.

     b **2♥**   If partner corrects to 2♠, you can suggest a game with 3♠.

     c **pass**   Good one for the method! You can play in diamonds.

     d **2NT**   You are willing to play in game, so look for a 5-3 fit in a major.

C H A P T E R

NAMYATS

Suppose you hold this rather nice collection:

♠ 7 2   ♥ A K Q 10 4   ♦ A J 6   ♣ K 7 3

Unfortunately, you are in third chair, and your partner opens the bidding with 4♠. Quick, what do you do now?

Of course, to some extent the kind of hand your partner is likely to have will vary with the vulnerability. But surely you must be at least tempted to look for a slam. If partner has seven solid spades, and perhaps even a side queen, 6♠ may not be a bad contract. On the other hand, if partner has opened on eight to the queen-jack (trying to make life difficult for the opponents) you may go down at the four-level. So what do you do?

The difficulty arises precisely because an opening bid of four of a major has a wide range. To address this problem, the inventors of Namyats decided to open relatively weak preemptive hands with 4♥ and 4♠, and to do something else with the stronger one-suited hands. They chose to make use of two opening bids that don't occur very often in their natural sense: 4♣ and 4♦.

What is Namyats?

An opening bid of 4♣ shows a strong preempt in hearts.
An opening bid of 4♦ shows a strong preempt in spades.

So, 4♣ shows a stronger hand than an opening bid of 4♥. What sort of hand will partner expect when you open 4♣? A typical Namyats hand will contain a solid eight-card trump suit or a one-loser eight-card trump suit and an ace outside, like these two examples:

♠ 8	♠ Q 4
♥ K Q J 10 8 7 5 2	♥ A K Q J 9 7 6 3
♦ 8 4	♦ 8 5
♣ A 10	♣ 6

Note that both these hands follow the basic requirement for a preemptive bid: you will make a lot of tricks if you choose trumps but very few if the opponents choose trumps. You get the picture, then. A Namyats opening shows relatively few points and about eight playing tricks.

The two hands above are classic examples of the opening. If you restricted its use to such precise specimens, you would not be making the best use of having two different bids for a four-level preempt. So, also open 4♣ on hands like these:

♠ K J	♠ 8
♥ A Q J 10 7 6 4 3	♥ A K Q J 7 6 3
♦ 4 3	♦ 9
♣ 9	♣ Q J 9 3

If instead you were to open 4♥, you would have a weaker hand, like these:

♠ 8	♠ 9
♥ K Q 10 8 7 5 4 2	♥ A K J 9 7 6 3
♦ J 10 3	♦ J 8 6 2
♣ 6	♣ 5

When you have something like a 15-count and seven or eight hearts, there is no real need to preempt. You can open 1♥ and proceed with the auction in a normal way. You would not open at the four-level on either of these hands, for example:

```
♠ 8                    ♠ 4
♥ A K Q 9 7 4 2        ♥ K Q J 10 7 6 4 3
♦ J 3                  ♦ A K 7
♣ A Q 6               ♣ 8
```

Both these hands have too much outside the heart suit for a preempt. The playing strength is also too great — you might miss a slam if partner has good values. Open both hands with a simple 1♥ and bid strongly thereafter.

How do you respond to 4♣ or 4♦?

Unless you see some prospects of a slam, you will normally respond by bidding four of opener's major suit.

♠ A 4 ♥ Q 4 ♦ K 10 8 7 2 ♣ K J 6 2

Partner	You
4♣	?

You respond 4♥ and play there. Partner has shown a preemptive opening, remember, not some variety of strong two-bid. If his hearts are headed by the ace-king, he will not hold an ace outside as well. You expect to lose to the minor-suit aces and might well lose a third trick somewhere too.

♠ A J 10 8 7 5 ♥ 6 ♦ J 8 6 4 ♣ Q 6

Partner	You
4♣	?

Again you respond 4♥. This does not show any heart support. You are merely converting partner's artificial bid into the contract that he has said he wants to play in. You can think of a Namyats 4♣ as a form of transfer bid. A response of 4♠ would be natural, to play in spades, but your spades are nowhere near good enough for this action here. Partner has at least seven hearts and probably eight. He may hold no spades at all.

When you have good support and a fair number of controls, you may suggest a slam by making the in-between bid (4♦ over 4♣, 4♥ over 4♦). Partner now defines his hand by cuebidding a side-suit ace or by rebidding 4NT with at least A-K-Q-x-x-x-x in the trump suit. When partner shows a side-suit ace, you may assume that there is only one likely loser in the trump suit when playing opposite a singleton in support.

Let's look at a typical auction where responder is interested in a slam:

Partner	You
♠ K Q J 9 8 6 5 3	♠ 7 2
♥ J 7	♥ A K Q 10 4
♦ 9	♦ A J 6
♣ A 2	♣ K 7 3
4♦	4♥
5♣	6♠

This is the example hand we started with. You have a source of top tricks to add to partner's advertised long spade suit. Opposite a Namyats 4♦ you suggest a slam by responding in the next suit up (4♥ here) and partner's 5♣ rebid shows the ace of clubs and a one-loser spade suit. That's what you want to hear, and you bid the slam. Even if partner had held two small diamonds, and a diamond was led against 6♠, there would still be a good chance of discarding the diamond loser on a surplus winner in your hand.

Suppose next that partner had rebid 4NT over 4♥, showing a solid spade suit. Again it would be reasonable for you to bid 6♠. The ♣K would be protected from the opening lead and, if partner held only seven spades instead of eight, the heart suit would be certain to offer some play for twelve tricks. Only if partner were to rebid 4♠ would you stay short of a slam. Such a rebid would indicate that partner did not have a classic 'solid spades, or one-loser spades and an ace' Namyats hand. He might, for example, hold:

♠ K Q J 9 8 6 5 2 ♥ 8 ♦ K Q ♣ 9 4

With eight playing tricks, he was worth a Namyats opening. However, a slam would be no good now. The defenders would have two cashable aces.

Suppose that partner had opened 4♠ instead of 4♦, showing a lesser hand:

Partner	You
♠ K Q J 9 8 6 5 4	♠ 7 2
♥ J 7	♥ A K Q 10 4
♦ 9	♦ A J 6
♣ 6 2	♣ K 7 3
4♠	?

Now you know what to do: you would pass. With a possible club lead coming through the king, the defenders might well take three tricks.

What should you do if 4♣ or 4♦ is doubled?

Nearly always you will simply bid four of partner's long suit over a double, whatever the double means. If instead you bid four of the in-between suit, this would still be asking for more information about the opener's hand. A pass would mean that you could see no advantage to becoming declarer on the hand. If the fourth player passed too, the opener would bid four of his suit, prepared to play the contract.

How do you respond to a 4♥ or 4♠ opening if you are playing Namyats?

In a word, the answer is 'cautiously'. Partner's preempt was aimed at making life difficult for the opponents. He may, for example, have opened a non-vulnerable 4♠ on this hand:

♠ Q J 10 7 6 5 4 2   ♥ 6   ♦ J 10 3   ♣ Q

If you carry him to the five-level on some abortive slam venture, and the contract goes one down, it will be your fault and not your partner's.

With this warning in mind, what do various responses mean? When the auction starts:

Partner	*You*
4♥	?

you might use these responses:

4♠	to play
4NT	Roman Keycard Blackwood, with hearts as trumps
5♣/5♦	cuebid that suggests a slam
5♥	asks partner to bid a slam with good trumps

When you invite a slam by raising to the five-level, how good should the opener's trumps be in order to accept? His suit should be playable for one loser opposite a singleton. So, he should accept with K-Q-J-x-x-x-x, even though he has only seven trumps. He should decline with K-J-10-x-x-x-x-x.

Summary

✓ Playing Namyats, a 4♣ opening shows a strongish preempt in hearts and 4♦ shows a similar hand with spades.

✓ A typical Namyats opening is based on a solid trump suit, or a one-loser trump suit with a side-suit ace.

✓ With two aces outside the trump suit, or one ace and a void, you should open 1♥ or 1♠ rather than with a Namyats bid. There is too much chance of missing a slam.

✓ In response to 4♣ or 4♦, a bid of the in-between suit invites a slam. Partner may then sign off in his suit, cuebid any side-suit control or rebid 4NT with solid trumps.

NAMYATS

NOW TRY THESE...

1   Playing Namyats, what would you open on each of these hands?

a   ♠ A K Q J 10 7 6 3
    ♥ J 7
    ♦ 10 5
    ♣ Q

b   ♠ A 8 2
    ♥ K Q J 10 9 6 3
    ♦ 3
    ♣ A 5

c   ♠ K Q J 9 8 6 4
    ♥ 5
    ♦ Q J 9 2
    ♣ 3

d   ♠ J 8
    ♥ K Q J 9 6 5 3
    ♦ 9 7
    ♣ 6 3

e   ♠ J 8
    ♥ A Q J 8 7 6 2
    ♦ A Q 2
    ♣ 3

f   ♠ 8
    ♥ K Q J 10 8 5 4 3
    ♦ A 10
    ♣ J 6

2   On each of the following hands partner has opened a Namyats 4♣. What will you respond?

a   ♠ A K Q J 5
    ♥ J 8 7 2
    ♦ K 9 6 3
    ♣ —

b   ♠ A K Q 4
    ♥ A 6 3
    ♦ K Q 9 7
    ♣ 10 5

c   ♠ 10 5 2
    ♥ —
    ♦ 9 4 2
    ♣ A Q J 10 7 6 3

d   ♠ A 9 5 3
    ♥ 7 2
    ♦ A K Q J 9
    ♣ A 3

3   On each of the following hands partner has opened 4♥. How will you respond?

a   ♠ A K 8 7 6 3 2
    ♥ 9
    ♦ Q 9 3
    ♣ A 8

b   ♠ A K 3
    ♥ K 10 7
    ♦ Q J 10 6
    ♣ A K 3

c   ♠ A K 7 5
    ♥ 7
    ♦ A 10
    ♣ A K Q 7 6 2

d   ♠ A 9
    ♥ Q 7
    ♦ A K Q J 7
    ♣ A J 10 8

ANSWERS

1 **a** **4♦** With a solid eight-card trump suit, you are too strong for 4♠.

   b **1♥** With two side-suit aces, you are too strong for any preempt.

   c **4♠** Great for a preempt but not strong enough for Namyats. (You are too strong for 3♠ with this shape and a good side suit.)

   d **3♥** With 7-2-2-2 shape, you are not strong enough to open at the four-level.

   e **1♥** You are too strong for a preempt and should open at the one-level.

   f **4♣** Perfect for Namyats.

2 **a** **4♦** A slam is possible and you should enquire about partner's hand. If he signs off in 4♥, you will pass. If he rebids 5♣, showing the ♣A, you will sign off in 5♥. If instead he shows solid hearts (4NT), or the ♦A (5♦), you will bid 6♥.

   b **4♦** Again a slam is possible. If partner rebids 5♣, showing the ♣A, the odds are good that you can make 6♥. If instead he rebids 5♦, showing the ♦A, you will sign off in 5♥. There will be two losers in clubs unless partner has a singleton club and there is no way to find out.

   c **4♥** No reason to pass, thinking that your clubs are better than partner's hearts. In any case, 4♥ is a game contract and may possibly succeed.

   d **4NT** Bid Roman Keycard Blackwood to see what trump honors partner has. If he has the ace, king and queen, you will bid 7NT. If he shows either one or two keycards (which must be top trump honors), you will bid 6♥.

3 **a** **Pass** You are not strong enough to investigate a slam. Nor is there the slightest reason to play in spades instead of hearts. Your ♠A-K will be useful cards in a heart contract.

   b **5♣** If partner cuebids 5♦ over your cuebid of 5♣, you will bid 6♥. Otherwise you will sign off in 5♥, expecting two diamond losers.

   c **5♥** This asks if partner's trumps will play for one loser opposite a singleton. If they will, he will bid 6♥.

   d **4NT** If partner has two top trumps, bid 7NT, otherwise stop in 6♥.

MORE
COMPLICATED

CHAPTER 9

MORE ABOUT STAYMAN

WHAT'S IN A NAME?

The famous Stayman convention was invented by… (no, caught you there!) *George Rapée*. Sam Stayman was George's partner at the time and it was he who publicized the method and became world-famous as a result. Let's not forget that Stayman was also a fine player with three Bermuda Bowl wins to his name.

Everyone knows the basic Stayman convention: when partner opens 1NT you respond 2♣ to look for a 4-4 fit in a major suit. That's pretty straightforward if you only have a four-card major (although you may not know how to show partner you have a really strong hand once you have found a fit). What about hands where you are 5-4 in the majors, though? If you transfer, you may lose your four-card suit in the auction; if you don't, how will partner know you have five of them? Not so easy, is it? For the solution, read on…

BY THE WAY

Stayman and Blackwood are the world's most famous conventions — by a mile. Inventing a popular convention is a good way to achieve immortality. What, you haven't heard of the 'Seagram Defense to 5♣ openings'? Nor have you any idea what the 'Bird Three-Way Redouble' is? Well, we'll just have to hope that people remember us for this book…

How do you bid with a moderate 5-4 hand?

This begs the question, 'what about weak 5-4 hands?' That's easily answered: you transfer to your five-card suit, and pass partner's response; don't mess around trying for perfection on weak hands, just get out in a safe spot. But if you have 8 points or so and would like to invite game in either a 5-3 or 4-4 fit (assuming you have one), what do you do?

We recommend that you start with Stayman, and if partner responds 2♦, then bid your five-card suit:

Partner	You
1NT	2♣
2♦	2♥

This sequence will then show a hand with four spades and five hearts, on which you want to invite to game (without the spades, you'd just transfer to hearts and then bid 2NT). With five spades and four hearts, you would rebid 2♠ instead.

Here is a typical auction:

Partner	You
♠ A Q 7	♠ K 10 8 6 2
♥ K 6	♥ A 9 7 3
♦ A 10 8 7	♦ 9 2
♣ K 9 6 2	♣ J 3
1NT (15-17)	2♣
2♦	2♠
3♠	4♠

You show game-invitational values, five spades and four hearts. The 2♠ rebid is non-forcing but since partner has three-card spade support and a useful-looking hand he raises to 3♠. You are sufficiently encouraged to attempt a spade game. Had partner held the ♣A instead of the ♣K, he would have bid 4♠ instead of 3♠ at his third turn.

When opener has a maximum, he is allowed to bid again even if he has no fit for responder's five-card suit:

Partner	You
♠ Q 10 7	♠ K 8 6 2
♥ K 6	♥ A J 10 7 3
♦ A K J 6	♦ 5 4
♣ K J 9 4	♣ 8 3
1NT (15-17)	2♣
2♦	2♥
2NT	3NT

The game is no certainty but with 25 points between the two hands, you want to be there.

What about 5-4 hands where you want to be in game?

What if you hold a game-forcing hand (9 points or more) with five cards in one major and four cards in another? It is possible to describe such hands with a transfer sequence (showing the five-card suit with a transfer and then bidding the four-card suit). In North America it is more popular to deal with these hands via Stayman. If opener shows a major, you have found a fit. If instead he rebids 2♦, denying a four-card major, you can bid your five-card major at the three-level — a sequence which shows 5-4 in the majors.

Partner	You
♠ A 7	♠ K J 8 5 2
♥ J 10 8	♥ K Q 7 3
♦ K Q 6 3	♦ J 9 4
♣ A Q J 5	♣ 8
1NT (15-17)	2♣
2♦	3♠
3NT	

Your 3♠ rebid is game-forcing. Here, since partner has only two spades, he chooses to play in 3NT.

A corollary of bidding 5-4 and 4-5 major-suit hands via Stayman (rather than by using a transfer sequence) is the meaning attached to your second bid in this auction:

Partner	You
♠ Q 3	♠ A K 10 7 6
♥ A J 10 4	♥ K Q 8 5 2
♦ K 8 7	♦ 4
♣ A J 5 3	♣ K 2
1NT (15-17)	2♥
2♠	3♥
4♣	4NT
5♥	6♥

Your 2♥ shows five spades, as normal. Although a second-round bid in a new suit would normally guarantee no more than four cards, the 3♥ rebid now shows five hearts. That's because with five spades and only four hearts you would have bid Stayman initially instead of using a Jacoby transfer. Since you would have rebid 4♥ if you simply wanted partner to choose a major suit at the game-level, you must be interested in a slam when you follow this path.

> **BY THE WAY**
>
> Some tournament players like to use the Smolen convention, in which the three-level bid is made in the four-card suit. Thus 1NT-2♣; 2♦-3♥ would show four hearts and five spades. This works a little like a transfer, since the 1NT bidder will end up on play in the 5-3 fit if there is one.

Opener would bid 3♠ at his third turn on any good hand with spade support. It follows that 4♣ must be a cuebid agreeing hearts as trumps. It shows a club control and says that his hand is suitable for a slam, should you be thinking of such a target. Now comes Roman Keycard Blackwood and the excellent slam is reached.

What if you have a 4-card major and a 5- or 6-card minor?

Actually, we discussed this in Chapter 5, but it won't hurt to do a quick recap here. When you follow a Stayman inquiry with 3♣ or 3♦, this is natural and game-forcing. Suppose you hold these cards:

♠ 5   ♥ A Q 7 4   ♦ K 7 2   ♣ A Q 10 6 3

Partner	You
1NT (15-17)	2♣
2♠	3♣

You start with Stayman, to discover if partner holds four hearts. When he denies such a holding, you continue with 3♣. This rebid is game-forcing and shows a five-card club suit.

The bidding will continue in natural fashion. Note that the opener should not woodenly bid 3NT when he has club support. You would not have mentioned your club suit unless you would be happy to hear it raised. With this shape and a modest 9-count, you would have kept your club suit under wraps and rebid 3NT instead.

If instead you held six clubs and four hearts, you would start with a transfer to clubs (see Chapter 5), intending to rebid in hearts.

How do you make a slam try after Stayman?

Let's suppose you are lucky enough to be dealt the following, and hear partner open 1NT:

♠ A Q 8 3   ♥ J 7 2   ♦ K 4   ♣ A Q 9 2

Partner	You
1NT	2♣
2♦	?

You start with Stayman, and partner rebids 2♦. What now?

On this hand, you're going to want to play in notrump, and you can invite partner to bid a slam with a simple, quantitative, raise to 4NT. This is not Blackwood, because no suit has been agreed (or even bid, in this case!).

Partner	You
1NT	2♣
2♦	4NT

Partner will then bid 6NT on a maximum (17-point) hand and pass 4NT on anything less.

But what if you find a fit?

♠ A Q 8 3   ♥ J 7 2   ♦ K 4   ♣ A Q 9 2

Partner	You
1NT	2♣
2♠	?

You know that a 3♠ bid by you is just invitational, while partner will (correctly) pass if you just bid 4♠. So what do you do next to agree spades and suggest a slam?

There is a lot of sophisticated technology available, including using three of the other major as an artificial slam try, or using jumps to the four-level as either splinters or cuebids (or even as natural bids in some situations), but the auctions that follow can get very complex, and go well beyond the intended scope of this book. There's also no real expert consensus on the 'right' way to use these jumps to the four-level. We suggest you explore the possibilities with your favorite partner and choose something that makes sense to you both.

With an unfamiliar partner, and without specific discussion, that leaves you with two bids here that you already know:

4♣   Gerber, asking for aces

4NT   quantitative

Yes, there's no question that there are many hands where just asking for aces won't tell you what you need to know to make a sensible slam decision. However, for now, just live with it. When you're ready to make your system more complicated, the machinery is all there waiting for you to discover it!

We attach the same quantitative meaning to 4NT after a transfer response (a sequence such as 1NT - 2♥ ; 2♠ - 4NT). You are inviting a slam with a non-forcing bid of 4NT. Partner already knows that your hand contains five spades, so he will be well-placed to decide the best final contract.

Summary

✓ When you rebid 2♥ (or 2♠) over a 2♦ response to Stayman, you show 4-5 (or 5-4) shape in the majors and game-invitational strength.

✓ When you follow your Stayman inquiry with a rebid of 3♣ or 3♦, this is natural and game-forcing, and shows a hand with five-card minor as well as a four-card major.

✓ When you rebid 3♥ over a Stayman 2♦ response, you show game-forcing values (at least), five hearts and four spades. A 3♠ rebid shows a similar hand with five spades and four hearts.

✓ When you jump to 4NT over a 2♥ or 2♠ Stayman response, this is a quantitative (invitational) bid. (The same is true following a Jacoby transfer, in an auction such as 1NT – 2♥ ; 2♠ – 4NT)

MORE ABOUT STAYMAN

NOW TRY THESE...

1   How do you plan to bid these hands opposite partner's 1NT, which shows
    15-17 points? (Assume you are playing Stayman and four-suit transfers as
    described in Chapter 5.)

a   ♠ J 9 6 3 2   b   ♠ A K J 5
    ♥ K 10 6 4   ♥ 7 4
    ♦ 7 3   ♦ K Q 10 8 6
    ♣ 8 4   ♣ A 7

c   ♠ K J 9 7 3   d   ♠ A 10 8 6
    ♥ Q J 7 6 2   ♥ A Q 10 7 6
    ♦ 5   ♦ J 8 2
    ♣ K 4   ♣ 7

e   ♠ Q 4   f   ♠ A Q 9 6 2
    ♥ A J 9 2   ♥ K J 10 7 3
    ♦ K 8 5   ♦ 4
    ♣ A 7 6 4   ♣ A J

g   ♠ 7 4   h   ♠ K 8 7 4
    ♥ A Q 9 8   ♥ A 9 7 5 2
    ♦ 8   ♦ J 3
    ♣ A K 10 7 6 3   ♣ J 4

2   What will you bid next on each of these hands?

    You   **Partner**
    1NT   2♣
    2♦   2♠
    ?

a   ♠ 10 4 2   b   ♠ K 9 2
    ♥ Q J 2   ♥ Q 6
    ♦ K Q 8   ♦ A K 3 2
    ♣ A Q J 4   ♣ A J 8 4

3   What will you bid next on each of these hands?

    You   **Partner**
    1NT   2♣
    2♦   3♥
    ?

a   ♠ Q J 6   b   ♠ K 10
    ♥ A 2   ♥ Q 9 6
    ♦ K Q 8 3   ♦ A K 3 2
    ♣ Q J 10 4   ♣ A J 8 4

ANSWERS

1 **a** **2♥** Remember that bidding Stayman and then 2♠ indicates game-try strength. On a weak hand you must just transfer into the long suit.

b **2♣** Start with Stayman, to look for a 4-4 spade fit. If partner rebids 2♥ or 2♦, continue with a forcing 3♦.

c **2♥** Your hand is of game-forcing strength with 5-5 in the majors. Show the five spades by transferring and then jump to 4♥ to offer partner a choice of games.

d **2♣** With a game-forcing 5-4 hand, start with Stayman. If partner rebids 2♥ or 2♠, raise to game in that suit. Otherwise bid 3♥ next to show a game-forcing hand that is 4-5 in the majors.

e **2♣** Start with Stayman. However, good as this hand is, it is not going to be enough for slam even opposite a 17-point opener. You will be content to play in 3NT or 4♥.

f **2♥** With a slam-invitational 5-5 hand in the majors begin with 2♥, to show the spades, and then rebid 3♥.

g **2♠** With a 4-6 hand, show the longer suit by transferring to clubs (see Chapter 5), intending to rebid 3♥.

h **2♣** This moderate 9-count is worth no more than a game-try sequence. Start with Stayman and rebid 2♥ over 2♦. If partner shows a four-card major, raise 2♥ to 4♥ and 2♠ to 3♠.

2 **a** **pass** You have three-card spade support but a hand that is completely minimum in every respect.

b **4♠** What a difference from the previous hand! You have a maximum, a ruffing value, a queen in partner's second suit (remember partner has four hearts, or he wouldn't have gone through Stayman) and three winners in his short suits. You are worth a leap to game.

3 **a** **3NT** Partner is showing five hearts and four spades, and you have no fit with either suit.

b **4♣** This time you do have a heart fit, and you have much too good a hand just to bid 4♥. You have honors in both partner's suits, a maximum opener, and top controls in the minors. Remember, your cuebid must agree hearts, as you have already denied a fit with partner's four-card spade suit.

EXCLUSION BLACKWOOD

WHAT'S IN A NAME?

 Easley Blackwood launched the original version of his ace-asking convention back in 1933. In these days of highly conventional bidding sequences, it is hard to believe that many players of that era objected to such an artificial bid. It was tantamount to cheating, they claimed, to be able to find out how many aces partner held!

The earlier book in this series, *25 Bridge Conventions You Should Know* (have we mentioned it before?), described Roman Keycard Blackwood, which is hugely popular with tournament players. Since Exclusion Blackwood is based on this convention, it is worth refreshing our memories on how it works.

Roman Keycard Blackwood

Once a trump suit has been agreed, 4NT is Roman Keycard Blackwood and asks for 'keycards'. The four aces are all keycards and so is the king of the agreed trump suit.

These are the responses to the 4NT inquiry:

5♣	1 or 4 keycards
5♦	3 or 0 keycards
5♥	2 keycards but no queen of trumps
5♠	2 keycards and the queen of trumps

Over the 5♣ or 5♦ responses the 4NT bidder may inquire about the queen of trumps. How is this done? By making the cheapest available bid that is not in the trump suit. Over a 5♣ response, for example, 5♦ would ask for the queen of trumps unless diamonds was the agreed trump suit. In that case 5♥ would ask for the queen of trumps.

How do you respond to the queen-ask bid?

Without the trump queen, you sign off at the lowest available level in the agreed trump suit. Any other response shows the trump queen. Since the three side-suit aces have already been located, the responder to the queen-ask cuebids his lowest side-suit king. If such a cuebid would be beyond six of the agreed suit, he responds 5NT instead. When the responder holds the trump queen but no side-suit king he will bid six of the trump suit.

Does that all sound a bit complicated? Yes! But it is well worth the effort to learn the convention. The king and queen of trumps are vital cards when it comes to bidding slams. You cannot afford to wait until dummy goes down to see whether the partnership has the top trumps that you need!

Before we discuss the subject of this chapter — Exclusion Blackwood — let's continue to refresh our memories by looking at some examples of basic Roman Keycard Blackwood.

Partner	You
♠ K 10 9 3	♠ A Q J 8 7 2
♥ A 8 4	♥ 5
♦ A J 10 8 2	♦ K Q 9
♣ 4	♣ K J 6

Partner	You
1♦	1♠
2♣	
5♦	4NT
	6♠

When you hear of a double fit, in spades and diamonds, you can tell that the playing strength is present to make twelve tricks. It's still essential to determine if the opponents can score two tricks first. You bid Roman Keycard Blackwood and hear that partner has 3 or 0 keycards. Since partner opened the bidding, he must surely hold 3 keycards. You do not much care whether partner has three aces, or two aces and the king of trumps. You are willing to try for twelve tricks in either case. If instead partner had shown only two keycards, you would have signed off in 5♠. A slam would then be at best on the trump finesse (if the other missing keycard was the trump king).

Are you getting impatient waiting to hear about Exclusion Blackwood? Your wish will soon be granted. We'll just see one example of the queen-ask bid first.

Partner	You
♠ A	♠ Q 8 3
♥ A 10 7 6	♥ K Q 9 5 2
♦ A Q 10 8 7 2	♦ K 4
♣ A K	♣ 10 8 6

Partner	You
2♣	2♥
4NT	5♣
5♦	6♦
7♥	

When partner hears a positive response in hearts, his thoughts immediately turn towards a slam. He bids Roman Keycard Blackwood (agreeing hearts as trumps since this is the only suit bid naturally). The 5♣ response shows one key-card, which must be the king of trumps. A grand slam is possible and partner continues with 5♦ — the first available bid that is not in the trump suit. This asks about the queen of trumps. Without this card you would sign off in 5♥ and partner would then raise to 6♥, which would become the final contract. Since you do hold the trump queen, you do not sign off. You bid your cheapest (in this case your only) side-suit king. That is just what partner wanted to hear — the queen of trumps and the king of diamonds. Heaven! He bids the grand slam, which will surely be made.

What is Exclusion Blackwood?

The great moment has come. Look at the bidding problem that this hand presents:

♠ Q J 7 5   ♥ K Q 10 5   ♦ A K Q 10 7   ♣ —

Partner opens 1♠ and you respond 2♦. What should you do next when partner rebids 2♠? What are your slam prospects? If partner has any two of these cards: ♠A, ♠K and ♥A, it will surely be worth bidding a small slam. If he has all three of those cards a grand slam will be there. But how can you find this out?

Suppose you bid 4NT, Roman Keycard Blackwood with spades agreed, and partner responds 5♥, showing two keycards. Not much help, is it? If one of his keycards is the ♣A you will have two potential losers in the major suits. If his two keycards are the ♠K and the ♣A, you would be missing two cashable aces! What you need is some convention that says to partner: 'Tell me how many keycards you have but do not count the ♣A as a keycard.' There is such a convention and it is called — you guessed it — Exclusion Blackwood.

When you might have bid 4NT but instead choose to jump to the five-level in some non-trump suit, your bid is Exclusion Blackwood. These are the possible inquiry bids:

5♣	how many keycards do you have, excluding the ♣A?
5♦	how many keycards do you have, excluding the ♦A?
5♥	how many keycards do you have, excluding the ♥A?
5♠	how many keycards do you have, excluding the ♠A?

The convention does not apply in the trump suit (obviously!), only the three side suits. The responses to Exclusion Blackwood are the same as those for standard RKCB:

1st step	—	1 or 4 keycards
2nd step	—	3 or 0 keycards
3rd step	—	2 keycards but no trump queen
4th step	—	2 keycards with the trump queen

What does '1st step' mean? It means the next available bid over the Exclusion Blackwood enquiry. So, over a 5♣ Exclusion Blackwood bid, 5♦ would be the first step and 5♥ would be the second step.

Here's the example hand we saw before:

♠ Q J 7 5　♥ K Q 10 5　♦ A K Q 10 7　♣ —

Partner	You
1♠	2♦
2♠	?

Playing Exclusion Blackwood, you can bid 5♣, asking for keycards not including the ♣A. If partner responds 5♠ (the third step), you will know that he holds two useful keycards. You can then bid a small slam. Holding the combination that we feared previously (the ♠K and ♣A), partner would respond 5♦ to show only one keycard, and you would sign off in 5♠.

BY THE WAY

*There are a few auctions where you can save space (and thereby reduce the risk of getting too high) by making the Exclusion Blackwood bid at the four-level. This is possible when you have agreed trumps at the three-level and you then **jump** to a different suit at the four-level.*

Can you still ask about the trump queen?

As with standard RKCB, you may follow up your Exclusion Blackwood bid with an inquiry about the trump queen. You do this by making the next available non-trump bid. (Space may be constricted since the initial keycard inquiry is usually higher than 4NT.)

Partner	You
♠ 10 5	♠ A K 4 3
♥ A Q J 7 6	♥ K 9 5
♦ K 6	♦ A Q J 9 7 3
♣ Q J 8 3	♣ —
1♥	2♦
2♥	5♣
5♦	5♠
6♦	7♥

Your 5♣ bid is Exclusion Blackwood, with hearts agreed as trumps. Partner's first-step response shows one useful keycard, which must be the ace of trumps. You are now prepared to play at the six-level, at least. If there happens to be a trump loser, the slam will still be likely to succeed if partner holds the ♦K or if the diamond finesse is right.

However, you have no reason to abandon the search for a grand slam. You continue with 5♠, the next available bid not in the trump suit. This asks partner if he holds the queen of trumps. The 6♦ response should bring a look of ecstasy to your face. It means 'Yes, I do have the trump queen, and also the ♦K.' With every expectation that both red suits will run, you can leap to the grand slam.

Had you continued with 5NT instead of 5♠, this would have been an inquiry for side-suit kings, again as in standard RKCB. In this case it would be an inquiry for 'useful kings'. You have already shown a club void, so the king of clubs cannot be of much value.

Summary

✓ When you might have bid 4NT (RKCB) but choose instead to jump to five of a non-trump suit, this is Exclusion Blackwood. For example, in the sequence 1♠ - 3♠ ; 5♦, the 5♦ bid is Exclusion Blackwood. It asks 'How many keycards do you hold, not including the ♦A?'

✓ Partner responds on the normal four-step scale:

1st step:	1 or 4 keycards
2nd step:	3 or 0 keycards
3rd step:	2 keycards but no trump queen
4th step:	2 keycards with the trump queen

✓ As with normal RKCB, the keycard inquiry may be followed by a trump-queen inquiry (next available bid not in the trump suit) or a king-inquiry (5NT, if available).

EXCLUSION BLACKWOOD

NOW TRY THESE...

Playing Exclusion Blackwood, what will your next bid be in each case?

1
♠ A K Q 2
♥ K Q J 10 7 6 3
♦ —
♣ J 5

You	Partner
1♥	3♥ (10-12)
?	?

2
♠ A K J 4
♥ —
♦ K Q 9
♣ A Q 10 7 4 3

You	Partner
1♣	3♣ (10-12)

3
♠ A Q 9 8 6 2
♥ K J 7 4
♦ —
♣ A 8 3

You	Partner
1♠	3♠ (10-12)
?	

4
♠ A Q 10 8 2
♥ K Q 8 6 3
♦ K Q 5
♣ —

You	Partner
	1♦
1♠	3♠
?	

5
♠ —
♥ K Q 4
♦ K Q 6 5
♣ K Q 10 8 7 2

You	Partner
	1♥
2♣	3♣
?	

6
♠ K J 10 4
♥ A Q 10 6 4
♦ 5
♣ A 10 2

You	Partner
1♥	1♠
3♠	5♣
?	

7
♠ K 7 2
♥ 10 7 4
♦ K Q 9 6 2
♣ K 5

You	Partner
	1♦
3♦	4♣
4NT	5♣
?	

8
♠ K J 10 7 4
♥ 8 3
♦ A 10 7 4
♣ 9 2

You	Partner
	1♠
4♠	5♣
?	

ANSWERS

1   **3♠**   It is not advisable to use any form of Blackwood when you have two top losers in one of the side suits (here clubs). Suppose you were to bid 5♦ and hear that partner held one keycard outside diamonds. This could easily be the ♥A, a card that you suspected partner held all along. You would have no idea whether you had two top losers in clubs. Instead you should cuebid 3♠, hoping that partner can cuebid 4♣. Then would be the moment to bid 5♦, Exclusion Blackwood.

2   **4♥**   Perfect for Exclusion Blackwood. Do not worry about the possible loser in spades. Partner must have some values to justify the double raise. If the slam happens to be on a spade finesse, the finesse may win!

3   **4♣**   You are not quite strong enough to bid Exclusion Blackwood. Suggest a slam by cuebidding 4♣.

4   **5♣**   Perfect for Exclusion Blackwood again, especially with a fit for partner's diamonds. If partner shows two useful keycards bid a small slam. If he shows three, go for the grand!

5   **4♠**   Exclusion Blackwood. If partner shows only one useful keycard, bidding 4NT, you will sign off in 5♣. Opposite two keycards, you will bid 6♣; opposite three keycards, you will... yes, bid the grand slam!

6   **5♠**   Partner's 5♣ is Exclusion Blackwood. You have two keycards outside the club suit (♠K and ♥A) and no queen of trumps. You must make the third-step response of 5♠.

7   **6♣**   Partner's 4♠ was Exclusion Blackwood. Since you had one useful keycard, you responded with the first step, 4NT. Partner's subsequent 5♣ is the next available bid not in the trump suit and therefore asks about the queen of trumps. Since you do hold that card you bid your cheapest useful side-suit king. You ignore the ♠K, since you know partner is void in that suit.

8   **5♦**   Partner's 5♣ is not a jump bid, so it is not Exclusion Blackwood. It is a control-showing cuebid, suggesting a spade slam. You have nothing to be ashamed of, as far as your hand is concerned, so you happily cooperate by cuebidding the ♦A.

C H A P T E R

INGBERMAN

WHAT'S IN A NAME?

 Monroe Ingberman made several contributions to bidding theory, particularly in the important area of showing a raise for partner's suit (splinter bids, fragment bids and inverted minor raises). A noted mathematician, he was a professor at the University of Chicago and Northwestern University.

You sit down with an unfamiliar partner and the bidding starts

Partner	You
1♦	1♠
2♥	

Partner has reversed, yes, and therefore shows 17 points or more with longer diamonds than hearts. That much is clear. Is 2♥ forcing? Years ago you might have received a few 'No' votes. Nowadays, nearly everyone plays a reverse as forcing for one round. Opposite a two-level response, everyone plays that a reverse is forcing to game, whether or not they play two-over-one as game-forcing in general. Now we come to the big question: after a start such as this, which continuations by responder are forcing?

There is no general agreement in this area and it is one of the matters you would have to discuss in a new partnership. By playing the Ingberman convention, you will know exactly which rebids are forcing and which are not, and can avoid the indignity of playing in a partscore when you hold 28 points between the two hands!

So what is Ingberman?

Partner	You
1♦	1♠
2♥	2NT

After a reverse facing a one-level response, responder's rebid of 2NT is Ingberman. It usually shows a weak hand that wants to sign off somewhere. Opener is requested to bid 3♣ and to pass if responder simply chooses one of his suits.

Let's see the method in action.

Partner	You
♠ 9 3	♠ A Q 7 2
♥ A Q 7 4	♥ J 8 3
♦ A K 10 8 2	♦ 7 6 3
♣ A 4	♣ 10 8 5
1♦	1♠
2♥	2NT
3♣	3♦
pass	

BY THE WAY

The situation is different when the first response is at the two-level. Since a sequence such as 1♥ - 2♣ ; 2♠ is game-forcing, a continuation of 2NT by responder is not Ingberman. It is natural and shows at least one stopper in diamonds, the unbid suit.

You are in the minimum range for a one-level response. Since your hand will not be good enough for game facing a minimum reverse, you rebid 2NT (Ingberman). As requested, partner rebids 3♣. Now your 3♦ is a sign-off in that suit and on this occasion partner does not have the extra values to bid any further. Suppose your diamonds had been Q-6-3 instead. With enough for game now, opposite a reverse, you would have bid 3♦ (forcing) instead of an Ingberman 2NT on the second round.

Let's see what happens when the opener is stronger. On this next hand partner has 19 HCP and decides to press for game anyway once you respond to his opening bid:

Partner	You
♠ 4	♠ K J 8 6
♥ A K 8 2	♥ 10 5 3
♦ K J 7	♦ Q 5 4
♣ A K J 9 2	♣ 6 5 3
1♣	1♠
2♥	2NT
3NT	

With an unimpressive 6-count you intend to sign off in 3♣, using an Ingberman 2NT for that purpose. On this occasion partner does not rebid 3♣, as requested, because you might (and would here) pass. With sufficient extra values to insist on a game contract, partner bids 3NT instead, and the best contract is reached. This is similar to the situation after a Jacoby transfer where opener is allowed to 'break' the transfer under some circumstances.

Now let's see what can happen when the responder is stronger.

Partner	You
♠ 4	♠ K 10 9 5 2
♥ A Q 8 2	♥ K J 5 3
♦ A K Q 7 6 2	♦ 5 4
♣ 9 8	♣ A 6
1♦	1♠
2♥	3♥
4♦	5♣
6♥	pass

If you had a miserable 6-count with four hearts, you would bid 2NT first and then retreat to 3♥ over partner's 3♣ bid. The direct raise to 3♥ is therefore forcing. Partner cuebids in diamonds to suggest a slam. You have good trump support and can feel justified in carrying the bidding beyond game with a cuebid of 5♣. Partner can now be confident that both the playing strength and the controls are present for a slam to be a good prospect.

Is a rebid of your own suit weak or strong?

As we have seen, when you play Ingberman a rebid by responder in one of opener's suits is forcing. A jump rebid of responder's own suit is obviously forcing too:

Partner	You
1♦	1♠
2♥	3♠

That leaves just one bid whose forcing nature may be debated — a rebid of responder's suit at the two-level. What do you make of this start to the auction:

	Partner	You
	1♦	1♠
	2♥	2♠

Some players treat your rebid as forcing, saying that all weak hands must bid an Ingberman 2NT to sign off. Suppose you hold these cards, though:

♠ K Q 8 7 2   ♥ 8 5 2   ♦ 9   ♣ 10 7 6 4

If 2♠ were played as forcing and you bid an Ingberman 2NT instead, what could you say over partner's 3♣ waiting bid? Would you bid 3♦ and play in a fit that may be no better than 5-1? Or play in a 4-3 heart fit? Or insist on playing in 3♠? What you would like to do is bid a non-forcing 2♠ and leave any further move to partner. So, our advice is to play a rebid of responder's suit at the two-level as non-forcing. All other rebids (except an Ingberman 2NT, of course) are game-forcing.

Playing 2♠ as non-forcing does not inconvenience you in the slightest when you are stronger. You can jump to 3♠ when you have a good six-card spade suit. When you have five spades and enough points for game, you can bid the fourth suit. That's what happens here:

Partner	You
♠ J 7 3	♠ A K 9 8 5
♥ A Q 8 2	♥ J 5
♦ A Q 10 9 6	♦ J 4
♣ A	♣ 9 7 6 4
1♦	1♠
2♥	3♣
3♠	4♠

Here you are too strong to bid 2♠, non-forcing, so you bid 3♣ (fourth suit forcing). Partner shows his three-card spade support and the par contract is reached.

What do you bid with a natural 2NT hand?

As always, when a convention takes away a useful natural bid, we must consider what to do with the hands previously covered by 2NT. What would you bid here:

Partner	You
♠ A 8	♠ Q J 4
♥ 10 6	♥ K 9 8 3
♦ A J 10 5	♦ 6 4 3
♣ A K J 8 2	♣ 10 7 6
1♣	1♥
2♦	?

If 2NT were natural, you might well choose that bid. What do you rebid when you are playing Ingberman? Since you are not strong enough to insist on game, you do best to bid an Ingberman 2NT, intending to pass 3♣. Sometimes you will be forced to take this route when you hold only a doubleton club. It doesn't happen very often, though, if you follow our recommendation that a simple rebid of responder's initial suit is non-forcing.

Add another two points or so to your hand and you would have enough for game. You could then bid 2NT (Ingberman), intending to continue with 3NT. If your stopper in the fourth suit was particularly secure, you could leap directly to 3NT, showing your confidence that this was the right contract.

Summary

✓ Opener's reverse opposite a one-level response is forcing for one round. When the responder is weak, he has two options: he may rebid his own suit at the two-level, or he may bid 2NT (Ingberman). All other rebids are forcing to game.

✓ When responder bids an Ingberman 2NT, opener is requested to rebid 3♣. He will do so unless his opening bid was 1♣ and he has sufficient extra strength to insist on game. In that case he must make some other bid.

✓ Responder's next bid after Ingberman is intended as a sign-off. Opener should pass unless he has substantial extra values.

✓ When responder has a stopper in the fourth suit, he should jump to 3NT only when that stopper is reliable. Otherwise he can express doubt on the matter by bidding an Ingberman 2NT, intending to bid 3NT on the next round.

INGBERMAN

NOW TRY THESE...

Playing Ingberman, what will your next bid be in each case?

1	♠ A K 10 8 2
	♥ 7 6 3
	♦ Q 5 2
	♣ 8 3

Partner	You
1♦	1♠
2♥	?

2	♠ 8 6 5
	♥ K 10 9 2
	♦ K 9 3
	♣ 10 7 4

Partner	You
1♣	1♥
2♦	?

3	♠ 9 2
	♥ K 7
	♦ A Q 7 2
	♣ A 10 9 6 3

Partner	You
1♥	2♣
2♠	?

4	♠ K 10 9 8 2
	♥ Q 8 6
	♦ 5
	♣ J 7 4 2

Partner	You
1♦	1♠
2♥	?

5	♠ A K 7 2
	♥ 10 4 3
	♦ J 5
	♣ A Q 10 7

Partner	You
1♣	1♠
2♦	?

6	♠ K Q J 10 4 3
	♥ J 10 5
	♦ 5 3
	♣ A 2

Partner	You
1♦	1♠
2♥	?

7	♠ A Q 9 5 2
	♥ 10 7 4
	♦ K 9 2
	♣ K 5

Partner	You
1♣	1♠
2♦	?

8	♠ 7 4
	♥ A J 8 5 3
	♦ A 10 7 4
	♣ 6 3

Partner	You
1♣	1♥
2♦	?

9	♠ K 5
	♥ 7 4
	♦ A Q 8 4
	♣ A K J 9 5

Partner	You
	1♣
1♠	2♦
2NT	?

10	♠ A J
	♥ 9 8
	♦ K Q 10 5
	♣ A K Q 6 4

Partner	You
	1♣
1♥	2♦
2NT	?

ANSWERS

1 3♦ You would bid 2NT (Ingberman) on a weak hand with diamond support, so 3♦ is forcing to game. Partner will now have the opportunity to show three-card spade support.

2 2NT If you bid 3♣, it would be game-forcing. On a weak hand, where you want to play in three of the opener's long suit, you rebid 2NT (Ingberman), intending to pass partner's 3♣ bid.

3 2NT Ingberman does not apply after a two-level response, since all sequences are forcing-to-game anyway. (That's because responder has shown 10+ and opener has shown extra values.) Here you are happy to bid a natural and forcing 2NT to seek further description of the opener's hand. You don't jump to 3NT, expressing confidence that this is the right contract, because there is some chance of a slam.

4 2♠ Be thankful that a rebid of your suit is non-forcing and shows a weak hand! The hand would be a nightmare otherwise.

5 4♣ A rebid of 3♣ is forcing and would not be a mistake. However, with such splendid club support and a slam beckoning, it is better to put partner in the picture with a jump bid.

6 3♠ A rebid of 2♠ would be non-forcing. Here you are too strong for that action and you have an excellent spade suit too. A bid of 3♠ conveys both these messages.

7 2♥ You have a strong hand and no idea where to play. This is the exactly the right time to use a conventional fourth suit forcing bid.

8 3♦ With 9 HCP, not to mention two fine aces, you are justified in forcing to game with this raise of partner's suit.

9 3♣ Partner probably wants to sign off in 3♣ or 3♦. By rebidding 3♣, you will allow him to do this.

10 3NT Again partner wants to sign off but you are reluctant to allow this when you hold a full 19 HCP yourself. Cross your fingers (if you think it will help!) and bid 3NT.

WEAK JUMP SHIFTS

W H A T ' S   I N   A   N A M E ?

 Like much of today's 'standard' bidding, the jump shift to show a very strong hand in response to an opening bid was originated by ***Ely Culbertson***. He had a different name for it, however: the 'jump takeout' or 'forcing takeout'.

In the early days of bridge the higher you bid, the stronger your hand was. An opening 2♥ was strong, an opening 3♥ was stronger! Nowadays, tournament players use both these bids to show a weak hand. Similarly, when partner opens 1♥ a response of 2♠ has always been stronger than 1♠. You will not be surprised to hear that some players now use weak jump shifts, showing a long suit and very few points.

Partner	*You*
1♥	2♠

The traditional meaning of a jump shift (like this example) is to show a very strong hand on which a slam might be possible. Although modern players restrict the hand types on which a strong jump shift may be made, it cannot be denied that such bids work well when they do come up. However, in this chapter we will look at a different possible use for the jump shift. When you come to deciding whether or not to play 'weak jump shifts' you will have to assess the value of the new method against the traditional usage. It is not as if you will be making good use of an otherwise unused bid here. You will be exchanging a handful of apples for a handful of oranges and you must decide which taste you like better.

So what is a weak jump shift?

A weak jump shift shows 3-6 HCP and a long suit. At the two-level a six-card suit is sufficient; at the three-level you need a seven-card suit.

Before discussing the claimed benefits of the scheme, let's look at some typical hands on which you might make such a response.

♠ Q J 10 4 3 2　♥ 8　♦ J 9 7　♣ 10 8 2

If partner opens 1♣, 1♦, or 1♥, you respond 2♠. Most of the time partner will pass this response. We will see later what he can do if he wishes to try for game, despite your announced weakness.

This is a typical weak-jump-shift hand based on a minor suit:

♠ J 8 2　♥ 9 2　♦ 5　♣ K J 10 8 7 3 2

BY THE WAY

If you play that 3♣ and 3♦ are weak jump shifts over a major-suit opening, this precludes the use of Bergen Raises (see Chapter 3).

Opposite an opening bid of 1♦ or 1♥ you respond 3♣. If instead partner opened 1♠, you would ignore the clubs and raise to 2♠.

You can see the type of hand that is required for a weak jump shift. It is the same as for a very weak opening preempt in the suit you will be bidding. When the response is at the three-level you will need a seven-card suit to justify bidding so high.

What advantages are claimed for this method? The main one is that you will make life more difficult for your left-hand opponent, when he has a strong hand and wants to enter the auction. Another advantage is that you describe your whole hand in one bid. Partner will have a good picture immediately and can choose his continuation accordingly.

There is also an indirect benefit when responder spurns a weak jump shift and responds at the one-level, making a simple rebid of his suit on the next round:

You	Partner
1♦	1♥
1♠	2♥

Suppose you are the opening bidder in this auction. Your partner has shown a minimum hand with six hearts but he chose not to respond with a (weak) 2♥ on the first round. What deduction can you make? If he would always respond

2♥ when he held six hearts and 3-6 HCP, he must hold 7-9 HCP when he follows this alternative sequence. So, weak jump shifts allow you to bid with slightly greater accuracy when responder rebids his suit at the two-level.

A final advantage of weak jump shifts is that you can respond on a weak hand without fearing that partner will carry you to the sky on a hand that is a misfit. Suppose he opens 1♣ and you hold:

♠ K J 10 9 7 6   ♥ 8 3   ♦ 9 6 2   ♣ 10 2

With such a great spade suit it feels right to make a response of some sort. Suppose you are not playing weak jump shifts and you risk a 1♠ response. We have all been there before. Partner reverses to 2♥ and you attempt to sign off in 2♠. Allowing you no leeway, he continues with 2NT or (worse) 3NT and you end with a minus score. 'I couldn't bid any less,' he will tell you. 'I had 19 points!'

When you respond with a weak jump shift of 2♠ on such a hand, partner will realize that his 19-count with a singleton spade is not as great a hand as he thought when he picked it up. He should allow you to play in 2♠.

So, these are the potential advantages for weak jump shifts:

(a) they may shut out the next player

(b) they describe your hand in one bid

(c) they give more definition to sequences like 1♦ - 1♠ ; 2♣ - 2♠

(d) they allow you to respond more safely on a weak hand with a long suit.

How does opener rebid facing a weak jump shift?

On nearly all hands you will pass partner's weak jump shift. Remember that the bid shows a very weak hand indeed — less than the strength required for an opening weak two-bid. After a start such as 1♦ - 2♠, you can invite a spade game by raising partner's suit.

	You		Partner
	♠ A 8 4		♠ Q 9 7 6 3 2
	♥ A Q 8 6 2		♥ 7
	♦ A J 7		♦ 9 4 3
	♣ K 6		♣ J 8 5
	1♥		2♠
	3♠		pass

You see the chance of a spade game but partner rejects the offer.

Sometimes opener can see a chance of game even when he does not have a fit for responder's suit:

	Partner		You
	♠ 4 3		♠ K 10 9 7 6 2
	♥ A J 9		♥ 7 3
	♦ A K J 10 7 6		♦ Q 4
	♣ A Q		♣ 10 8 5
	1♦		2♠
	2NT		3NT
	pass		

Partner rebids 2NT, asking you to raise to game when you are at the top of your announced 3-6 HCP range. On this hand, you have good cards for him (the ♦Q, for instance, you expect to be valuable, as indeed it is) and 3NT has a pretty good play.

If instead the opener rebids his own suit, this is non-forcing and to play:

♠ A J 9   ♥ —   ♦ A K J 10 7 6 4   ♣ A 5 3

	You	Partner
	1♦	2♥
	3♦	

When the opener bids a new suit in an auction like this:

♠ 10   ♥ A K J 10 7 6   ♦ —   ♣ A K 10 7 5 2

	You	Partner
	1♥	2♠
	3♣	

the 3♣ bid is forcing. How else can you show a powerful two-suiter? You can always pass 2♠ with a lesser hand. This principle applies with even greater force after a three-level jump shift:

	You	Partner
	1♠	3♣

A rebid of 3♦ or 3♥ is forcing. Unless you have game in mind, with a splendid two-suiter of your own, you can always pass and play in partner's seven-card club suit.

If your right-hand opponent chooses the wrong moment to venture a bid over partner's weak jump shift, a double by you is (of course) for penalties.

♠ A K 10 6 2   ♥ K Q 2   ♦ A 10 9 4   ♣ 2

LHO	Partner	RHO	You
			1♠
pass	3♣	3♦	?

You wince when partner responds 3♣. An altogether different expression is appropriate when RHO enters the auction! You double for penalties.

Do weak jump shifts still apply if the opponents bid?

LHO	Partner	RHO	You
1♦	dbl		2♠

Yes, you can play weak jump shifts over a double. Whether you should is another matter. Remember that the doubler has suggested good holdings in three suits that include the one you are planning to bid. Also, if you play sequences like 1♥ - dbl - 3♦ as weak, you exclude the use of this bid as a Bergen Raise (see Chapter 3) or as a fit-showing jump (see Chapter 14).

LHO	Partner	RHO	You
1♥	1♠		3♣

If they overcall, as in this example, you can still play your bid as weak and natural if you want. Again this will preclude the use of such bids as Bergen Raises or fit-showing jumps.

How do you bid old-fashioned strong jump shift hands?

As we mentioned at the start of the chapter, you cannot evaluate weak jump shifts only by looking at hands where the responder has 3-6 points and a long suit. You must also consider those situations where you would previously have used a traditional strong jump shift. Will you be able to find satisfactory alternative auctions on such hands?

Suppose partner opens 1♥ and you hold:

♠ A K Q J 9 7   ♥ 8 3   ♦ A Q 2   ♣ Q 2

Playing strong jump shifts you would respond 2♠ and rebid 3♠, showing a great spade suit and suggesting a slam. If you are playing weak jump shifts, life is not so pleasant. After a start of:

Partner	You
1♥	1♠
2♣	

a rebid of 3♠ is not forcing (it shows about 10-12 points and invites game). So, you would have to bid 2♦ (fourth suit forcing) and rebid spades on the next round. This would not paint such a clear picture for partner.

The other classical use of a strong jump shift is when you have strong support for partner's suit:

♠ 9 7   ♥ A Q 8 3   ♦ A   ♣ A K J 8 7 2

Opposite 1♥ you would respond 3♣. If partner rebid 3♥ you could then cuebid 4♦ to agree partner's suit and suggest a slam. You don't lose so much here because after 1♥ - 2♣ ; 2♥ you can agree that a jump to 4♦ carries the same message. (If you play that a 2♣ response is game-forcing, there are no problems at all, and weak jump shifts do fit extremely well into a two-over-one system.)

So, we have outlined the potential advantages and disadvantages of weak jump shifts. The decision on whether to play them is, as always, up to you.

Summary

✓ A weak jump shift shows 3-6 HCP and at least six cards in the suit that you bid (seven cards at the three-level). The objective is two-fold: to describe your hand in one bid and to preempt the opponent who is next to speak.

✓ When opener can still see a chance of game, after a sequence such as 1♦ - 2♠, he may rebid 2NT (inviting game in notrump) or 3♠ (inviting game in spades).

✓ A rebid in opener's suit (such as 1♦ – 2♥ ; 3♦) is non-forcing. If opener rebids in a new suit (a sequence such as 1♥ - 2♠ ; 3♣), this is forcing. With a moderate two-suiter, opener should pass over the weak jump shift.

✓ You can use weak jump shifts over an intervening double or overcall, but remember that this will preclude the use of such bids as Bergen Raises or fit-showing jumps.

✓ Weak jump shifts fit extremely well into a two-over-one game-forcing system, where there is no need to use a strong jump shift.

WEAK JUMP SHIFTS

NOW TRY THESE...

1 You are playing weak jump shifts and partner opens 1♦. How would you respond on these hands:

a ♠ K Q 10 7 6 3
    ♥ 7
    ♦ J 3
    ♣ 10 4 3 2

b ♠ Q 9 7 2
    ♥ Q 10 9 7 3 2
    ♦ Q 3
    ♣ 9

c ♠ 10 4
    ♥ J 7 6 5 4 2
    ♦ 7 2
    ♣ K 9 3

d ♠ Q 9 2
    ♥ 8 5
    ♦ 7 2
    ♣ K J 7 6 5 3

2 Suppose you are playing weak jump shifts and partner opens 1♠. What would you bid on each of these hands?

a ♠ J 4 3
    ♥ 8
    ♦ 7 6
    ♣ K Q 10 6 4 3 2

b ♠ 9 2
    ♥ J 9 8 6 5 4 2
    ♦ 7 2
    ♣ K 9

c ♠ 7 4
    ♥ 8 5
    ♦ J 6
    ♣ Q J 10 6 4 3 2

d ♠ 2
    ♥ K Q 10 8 6 5 4
    ♦ 7 5 2
    ♣ 9 4

3 You open 1♦ and partner responds 2♥ (weak). What will you do next on each of these hands?

a ♠ K 5
    ♥ J 8 7
    ♦ A 10 9 8 5 3
    ♣ A K

b ♠ A 4
    ♥ A K 3
    ♦ A Q 10 9 4
    ♣ J 10 4

c ♠ Q 8
    ♥ 7
    ♦ A K 10 7 2
    ♣ A K J 9 6

d ♠ 5
    ♥ K Q 7 2
    ♦ K Q J 9 3
    ♣ A 3 2

ANSWERS

1 **a** 2♠ Perfect! A six-card spade suit with all your values packed into the suit.

b 1♥ You would not open with a weak 2♥ because of the four-card side suit in the other major. Similarly, you should not respond 2♥. (There are some renegades who would open 2♥, we realize!)

c 2♥ It's not perfect, with such a weak suit, and you would probably pass when vulnerable. However, if you play weak jump shifts you should look for excuses to use the bid, not reasons to pass.

d 1NT A 3♣ response requires a seven-card suit.

2 **a** 2♠ If you respond 3♣ instead you risk missing a spade game.

b pass You wouldn't open 3♥ on such a weak suit, nor should you respond 3♥. You don't agree and have always fared excellently making preempts on jack-high suits? Hmmm… can we play for money?

c 3♣ Perfect for the method. You have a good suit and no defense whatsoever to any contract by the opponents. They will not find it so easy to bid over 3♣.

d 3♥ The sort of hand that makes you glad you agreed to play weak jump shifts! All your strength is in the suit you are bidding.

3 **a** pass Even if partner holds a healthy ♥K-Q-x-x-x-x, you have no reason to expect to make ten tricks. When his hearts are less robust, you may be very happy to have stopped at the two-level. Remember that you are not facing a 6-9 HCP weak two-bid. Partner has at best 6 HCP.

b 3♥ Now you are stronger and will be willing to play in game if partner has an upper-range hand.

c pass Whether or not a rebid of 3♣ would be forcing (we recommend that it should be forcing), you have no reason whatsoever to disturb 2♥. Pass smoothly, and maybe the opponents will bid.

d 4♥ The opponents' silence, with such a big spade fit, is mystifying. Keep them quiet by raising to game. Partner might even make it.

SUPPORT DOUBLES

W H A T ' S   I N   A   N A M E ?

 The Support Double is among many conventions devised by one of the most outstanding bidding theorists in the history of the game — ***Eric Rodwell***. He and his regular partner, Jeff Meckstroth, are among the handful of players who have won all three major world titles: the Bermuda Bowl, the Olympiad and the Open Pairs.

The Support Double is a convention designed to tell you how many trumps the partnership holds in some competitive situations. Before looking at the convention in detail we should spend a brief moment looking at why this piece of information is so important.

The Law of Total Tricks

When a partscore auction becomes competitive, how high should you bid? Suppose your side has a high card or two to spare, for its bidding so far. Does this mean that you should bid one level higher when the opponents contest the auction? Not necessarily, because those high cards would also perform well in

SUPPORT DOUBLES

defense. What does affect your decision is the total number of trumps that your side holds. Let's look at a typical deal where one side holds spades and the other has hearts:

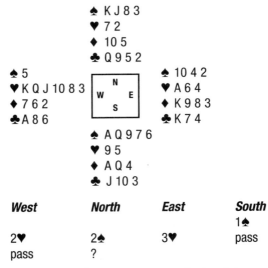

♠ K J 8 3
♥ 7 2
♦ 10 5
♣ Q 9 5 2

♠ 5
♥ K Q J 10 8 3
♦ 7 6 2
♣ A 8 6

♠ 10 4 2
♥ A 6 4
♦ K 9 8 3
♣ K 7 4

♠ A Q 9 7 6
♥ 9 5
♦ A Q 4
♣ J 10 3

West	North	East	South
			1♠
2♥	2♠	3♥	pass
pass	?		

BY THE WAY

Back in Chapter 3 on Bergen Raises, we recommended that you should bid immediately to the three-level when holding four-card support for partner's major-suit opening. This was an idea based on the Law of Total Tricks.

On competitive deals of this type, where the points are evenly divided, both sides should be willing to bid to the level dictated by the total number of trumps held. Here East-West hold nine hearts between them, so they should be willing to bid to the nine-trick level in hearts. As the cards lie, 3♥ will go one down against best defense (the defenders must set up their club trick before declarer establishes a discard on the diamond suit). It will be in a good cause, though, because 2♠ makes easily the other way.

North-South have nine trumps between them too, so on the auction shown North should be willing to bid 3♠. With the ♦K onside 3♠ will be made, as it happens. Suppose West held the ♦K, though. It would still be worth bidding 3♠, and going one down, because now 3♥ would succeed!

Suppose, instead of moving the ♦K from one side to the other, that we give East-West an extra honor card. If East (instead of North) holds the ♣Q, East-West will score an extra trick whether the deal is played in hearts or spades. It will again be worthwhile for North-South to bid to 3♠, going one down, because East-West would then have made 3♥.

One deal proves nothing, but you get the general idea. On competitive deals, it is the number of trumps you hold that determines how high you should be willing to bid. This general rule is one aspect of the Law of Total Tricks, which states that the total number of tricks that both sides can make, playing in their respective best fits, is usually equal to the total number of trumps held by the two sides.

On the deal we have been studying the total number of trumps held was 9 (North-South's spades) plus 9 (East-West's hearts) — a total of 18. So, the Law of Total Tricks suggests that about 18 tricks can be made. How these will be divided between the two sides will depend on (a) which side has more of the high cards and (b) whether or not the finesses are destined to win. If the cards are evenly divided, perhaps they can make 9 tricks each. If North-South have slightly the better of the cards, perhaps they can make 10 and East-West can make only 8. The total will still be 18.

After this lengthy but quite important preamble, we are going to look at a convention that allows responder to know whether opener has three-card or four-card support for his suit. It is known as the Support Double.

What is a Support Double?

You open one of a suit and partner responds in a major at the one-level. When your right-hand opponent enters the auction with an overcall, and the level of the bidding is such that you have the opportunity to raise partner's suit to the two-level, a double by you is a Support Double. It shows precisely three-card support for your partner. Suppose this is your hand:

♠ K 7 ♥ A 10 5 ♦ 9 4 ♣ A Q 10 6 4 3

LHO	Partner	RHO	You
			1♣
pass	1♥	1♠	dbl

You double to show three-card heart support. You would make the same call on all hands with three hearts — however weak or strong your hand was, and whatever shape you had in the other suits. You will have an opportunity on the next round to reveal your strength. For the moment partner will know that you have precisely three-card heart support. If instead you were to raise directly to 2♥ (or 3♥), he would know that you held four-card support. If you make any other call, such as Pass or 2♣, you deny three-card heart support.

How high do Support Doubles apply?

The Support Double applies when you have the opportunity to give a two-level single raise instead. In other words, the interference is below two of responder's suit. Why don't Support Doubles apply higher, as most types of doubles do? Suppose you hold this hand:

♠ 9 7 ♥ K 9 3 ♦ A Q 8 6 3 2 ♣ K 2

LHO	Partner	RHO	You
			1♦
pass	1♥	2♠	?

It would not be very comfortable if you had to double at this level whenever you held three-card heart support. You might well end up in 3♥, which would be too high if partner has only six points and a four-card heart suit. Over a jump overcall, when you do not have the opportunity for a single raise of partner's suit, a double reverts to its normal meaning in your system. Some players treat such a call as a penalty double; others would use it to indicate that they have extra strength but no convenient natural bid to make. On the present hand you would pass over 2♠.

How does the bidding continue?

When you hold a five-card suit in combination with partner's announced three-card support, a satisfactory trump suit has been found. You may sign off in the suit, invite game or bid game. For example:

♠ A 7 ♥ A Q 9 5 2 ♦ K 10 4 ♣ 10 6 4

LHO	Partner	RHO	You
	1♦	pass	1♥
2♣	dbl	pass	?

You rebid 4♥, bidding game in the 5-3 fit. Without the ♦K you would invite game by bidding 3♥. Take away an ace and a king and you would sign off in 2♥.

When you hold only four cards in the suit you have bid, you will usually seek a resting spot elsewhere:

♠ Q 8 5 2 ♥ K 10 8 3 ♦ Q 6 ♣ A 4 2

LHO	Partner	RHO	You
	1♦	pass	1♥
2♣	dbl	pass	?

Here you would rebid 2NT, inviting game. Without a club stopper, or any support for partner, you may sometimes have to rebid a four-card heart suit, but it should be done only as a last resort.

What if both defenders have bid?

As long as the conditions for a Support Double are met (i.e. you have the option of a single raise at the two-level), it makes no difference if both defenders have bid. A double will still show three-card support, as here:

♠ 9 6 2 ♥ K 6 3 ♦ Q 4 ♣ A K J 8 3

LHO	Partner	RHO	You
			1♣
1♦	1♥	2♦	?

You double to show your three-card heart support. Any other call — such as 2♠, 2NT, 3♣ or a pass — would deny three-card heart support. As before, a direct raise to 2♥ or 3♥ would promise four-card support.

The Support Redouble

When the opponent in the fourth seat makes a takeout double, you give the message of three-card support for your partner with a Support Redouble. Once again, any other bid or a pass will deny three-card support.

♠ A 10 7 2 ♥ J 8 4 ♦ A K Q 7 5 ♣ J

LHO	Partner	RHO	You
			1♦
pass	1♥	dbl	redbl

You redouble to show any hand with three-card heart support. Suppose on this hand partner had responded 1♠ instead of 1♥. You would then raise spades directly, to show four-card support. With the hand in this example, you would raise to 3♠.

Summary

✓ A Support Double, by the opener after an overcall by the player in the fourth seat, shows three-card support for responder's suit. The convention applies when the opener has room to make a single raise of partner's major suit at the two-level.

✓ If opener raises responder's suit directly, when he might instead have made a Support Double, he guarantees four-card support.

✓ When opener declines to make a Support Double, passing or bidding some other suit instead, he denies three-card support.

✓ When responder has five cards or more in his suit, he has found a satisfactory trump suit. He may sign off, invite game or bid game. When he holds only four cards in his suit he should usually warn his partner of this by seeking a different place to play.

✓ When the fourth player doubles instead of making an overcall, opener uses a Support Redouble to show three-card support.

SUPPORT DOUBLES

NOW TRY THESE...

1 Playing Support Doubles, what do you rebid on each of these hands?

LHO	Partner	RHO	You
			1♦
pass	1♥	2♣	?

a
♠ J 4
♥ K 10 3
♦ A 10 9 8 7 3
♣ A 5

b
♠ A K 5
♥ A 8 2
♦ K Q J 8 6 2
♣ 2

c
♠ A 10 3
♥ 7
♦ A Q 10 6 2
♣ A Q 9 4

d
♠ A 10 7 4
♥ K J 9 3
♦ A 7 6 2
♣ 6

2 What will you bid next on each of these hands?

LHO	Partner	RHO	You
	1♦	pass	1♥
1♠	dbl	pass	?

a
♠ Q 10 5
♥ J 9 7 6 2
♦ K J 4
♣ 10 3

b
♠ A Q 8 3
♥ K 10 7 2
♦ 9 3
♣ Q 10 5

c
♠ 10 5 3
♥ A 10 8 6 3
♦ J 4
♣ A J 7

d
♠ 10 9 2
♥ A J 7 2
♦ A 10 9 4
♣ Q 5

3 What will you bid next on each of these hands?

LHO	Partner	RHO	You
			1♥
pass	1♠	2♣	dbl
pass	2♥	pass	?

a
♠ A 10 5
♥ A Q 10 7 6
♦ 4
♣ A 10 6 3

b
♠ Q 8 3
♥ K J 10 9 7 2
♦ A 3
♣ A 5

c
♠ K 7 6
♥ A K J 8 3
♦ J 4
♣ A Q 7

d
♠ J 10 2
♥ A K J 7 2
♦ A Q 10 9 4
♣ —

ANSWERS

1 **a** dbl You show your three-card support. If partner has a minimum hand with only four hearts, you will have a safe resting place in 2♦.

   b dbl You make exactly the same call with a much stronger hand. If partner signs off, you will bid again.

   c pass You would like to make a penalty double (and are probably regretting the day when you read about Support Doubles!). All you can do is to pass and hope that partner reopens with a takeout double, which you will pass.

   d 2♥ With four-card support you raise partner's suit directly. Here you have a minimum opening bid and a raise to just 2♥ is appropriate.

2 **a** 2♥ You have found a 5-3 fit but you do not have the strength to invite a game. Bid 2♥ and leave any move towards game to your partner.

   b 2NT You do not want to play in a 4-3 heart fit, so you must look for some other place to play. With 11 points and two stoppers in the enemy suit, 2NT is just right!

   c 3♥ You are too strong to sign off in 2♥ and should invite game by jumping to 3♥.

   d 3♦ Only a 4-3 heart fit again but here you have an easy bid available in 3♦.

3 **a** pass Partner has signed off and is quite likely to hold only two hearts, so prospects of game are poor.

   b 3♥ You have a 6-2 heart fit at least, a secondary fit in spades and two aces. Since game will be possible opposite various 8-counts that partner may hold, you are worth one game try.

   c 2NT With 18 HCP you can hardly pass partner's sign-off. Since you have a double stopper in the enemy suit, the best move forward is 2NT.

   d 3♦ Game is still possible and 3♦ completes a description of your hand.

C H A P T E R 14

FIT-SHOWING JUMPS

W H A T ' S   I N   A   N A M E ?

 The idea of the fit-showing jump was first proposed by the late *Ed Manfield* in an article for *The Bridge World*. Manfield collected sixteen North American championships and two Rosenblum Cup medals in his distinguished career.

When the opponents get into the auction over partner's opening bid, you will virtually never have a hand that qualifies for a classic strong jump shift. We have already seen (Chapters 3 and 12) that even without the opponents being in the auction, modern players have new uses for this bid. There are several situations in competitive bidding where a jump in a new suit can be employed to show a fit for your partner – unimaginatively, this is known as a fit-showing jump (FSJ for short). One common situation occurs when your partner's opening bid has been doubled for takeout, and that will be our first topic.

Fit-showing jumps over a takeout double

Suppose you hold this hand:

♠ 9 2 ♥ Q 10 8 7 ♦ A Q 9 7 2 ♣ J 5

LHO	Partner	RHO	You
	1♥	dbl	?

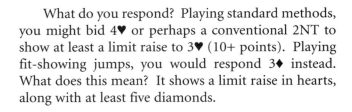
What do you respond? Playing standard methods, you might bid 4♥ or perhaps a conventional 2NT to show at least a limit raise to 3♥ (10+ points). Playing fit-showing jumps, you would respond 3♦ instead. What does this mean? It shows a limit raise in hearts, along with at least five diamonds.

How good do the two suits have to be to qualify for a FSJ?

When the opening bid is in a major suit and has promised five cards, you are allowed to make a fit-showing jump with only three trumps in support. They should be headed by the ace, king or queen in that case. As for the five-card side suit, it should be a good one and will usually be headed by two of the three top honors. It is up to you to decide whether to stick closely to these guidelines or to make fit-showing jumps more freely, whenever it seems that such a bid will best define your hand.

In general: a jump in a new suit over their takeout double shows four-card support for partner's suit (rarely, three to a top honor) and a good five-card holding in the suit you bid.

What is the point of such a bidding method? It makes life much easier for your partner if he is later faced with a high-level bidding decision. Suppose the bidding in our earlier example continues in this fashion:

♠ 9 2 ♥ Q 10 8 7 ♦ A Q 9 7 2 ♣ J 5

LHO	Partner	RHO	You
	1♥	dbl	3♦
4♣	?		

1)
♠ J 8 3
♥ A K J 6 2
♦ K 10 7 3
♣ 4

2)
♠ 10 7
♥ A K J 5 3
♦ 8 3
♣ A 10 9 3

If he has Hand 1, partner knows that there is a double fit in the red suits, and will bid on to 5♥. Opposite your actual hand, 5♥ will go only one down, with the enemy spade game a near-certainty to succeed. The situation changes on Hand 2. Since partner is short in diamonds and expects you to be short in clubs, it is clearly right to defend against 4♠. He will double and hope to pick up a worthwhile penalty.

One of the first things to ask, when considering a new convention, is: what will we lose by playing this? Playing fit-showing jumps over a double does prevent you from using Bergen Raises or weak jump shifts in this situation. You must decide which method you prefer.

BY THE WAY

If you liked weak jump shifts, which we described in Chapter 12, you will have to make a choice in some situations between playing them and playing fit-showing jumps.

Fit-showing jumps over an opponent's overcall

It is also worthwhile playing fit-showing jumps when there has been an overcall after your partner's opening bid. Suppose you hold this hand:

♠ K982 ♥ 107 ♦ KQ972 ♣ J5

LHO	Partner	RHO	You
	1♠	2♣	?

You have a hand worth a limit raise to 3♠, one that you would perhaps normally indicate with a cuebid of 3♣. Playing fit-showing jumps, it is more accurate to describe the hand with a bid of 3♦. As before, partner will then be better placed to make any high-level decision that comes his way. How many times in the past have you or your partner made the wrong decision in a competitive auction, saying afterwards 'Well, we had a double fit, but there was no way of knowing.' Now you will know if you have a double fit and can compete more aggressively when this is the case.

Sometimes, when partner has a big hand, your fit-showing jump will allow him to diagnose a slam.

	Partner	You
	♠ A K 10 8 6 2	♠ Q J 3
	♥ A 6 3	♥ J 9
	♦ K J 6	♦ A Q 10 4 3
	♣ 8	♣ 10 6 3

LHO	Partner	RHO	You
	1♠	2♣	3♦
pass	4NT	pass	5♣
pass	6♠	all pass	

Your 3♦ response announces a good diamond side suit and spade support that will be at least Q-x-x or x-x-x-x. It does not take a genius to realize that six spades, five diamonds and the ♥A will produce a small slam. Since there are no prizes for the brevity of auctions, it costs partner nothing to bid 4NT, checking that you do indeed have the expected ace of diamonds. If you held the ♣A too, a grand slam might even be there.

(Don't you just hate it when the writers of bidding books choose hands that illustrate how wonderful their suggested methods are?)

Does this mean you have to give up splinter bids?

Are you a fan of splinter bids (a response such as 1♠ - 4♣, showing a good spade raise and at most one club)? If your answer is 'Yes' you are in good company. They are widely used around the world. If you had to give up splinter bids to make way for fit-showing jumps, we would expect a fairly long and animated argument before convincing you! Fortunately the two methods can live happily alongside each other in many cases.

Where there is space for both a single jump and a double jump, the lower bid will be a fit-showing jump and the higher one a splinter bid. When partner opens 1♠ and there is a 2♣ overcall, this would be a typical scheme:

3♣	at least a limit raise to 3♠ (10+ points)
3♦/3♥	fit-showing jump
3♠	preemptive
4♣/4♦/4♥	splinter bid
4♠	preemptive

If you held a long heart suit and wanted to play in 4♥, you would bid a forcing 2♥ on the first round and then rebid 4♥.

What happens when there is not enough space for both a fit-showing jump and a splinter bid? You and your partner must take your pick between the two! Suppose the auction starts like this:

LHO	Partner	RHO	You
	1♠	2♥	?

Now 3♣ and 3♦ are needed as a natural bids, so only 4♣ and 4♦ are available as either fit-showing jumps or splinters. Our preference is to use the only available bid as a splinter bid, in such circumstances, but there is little to choose between the two methods. You must decide with your partner what you wish to do.

Fit-showing jumps facing an overcall

Another situation where fit-showing jumps are useful is when partner has made an overcall.

♠ K 10 6 2   ♥ Q 7   ♦ 10 2   ♣ K Q 7 5 2

LHO	Partner	RHO	You
1♦	1♠	pass	?

You can describe your hand nicely with a fit-showing jump of 3♣. Once again, the alternative call of 4♣ would be a splinter bid, showing at most one club.

The bids of 3♣ and 4♣ would have exactly the same meaning if RHO had made a negative double instead of passing over partner's spade overcall.

Summary

✓ A jump in a new suit, when partner has opened the bidding and RHO makes a takeout double or an overcall, is fit-showing. You show at least a limit raise of partner's suit (10+ points) and a five-card side suit headed by two of the three top honors.

✓ A jump in a new suit, facing an overcall by partner, is a fit-showing jump.

✓ When there is space for both a single jump and a double jump, you can make either a fit-showing jump or a splinter bid. When there is room only for a single jump, you need to agree with your partner which meaning the bid should have.

FIT-SHOWING JUMPS

NOW TRY THESE...

1 Playing fit-showing jumps, what will you bid on each of these hands?

	LHO	*Partner*	*RHO*	*You*
		1♠	dbl	?

a
♠ A Q 6 3
♥ K 7
♦ J 10 8 5 3
♣ 8 4

b
♠ Q J 8 3
♥ J 10 6
♦ 6
♣ K Q 9 7 3

c
♠ K 10 8 4 3
♥ K J 7
♦ 4
♣ K 9 8 5

d
♠ Q 7 2
♥ 5 2
♦ A Q 9 8 3
♣ Q 6 4

2 This time there is an overcall on your right.

	LHO	*Partner*	*RHO*	*You*
		1♥	2♣	?

a
♠ 7 2
♥ K J 9 8
♦ A Q 9 5 4
♣ 6 3

b
♠ K J 10 9 5
♥ J 10 6 4
♦ A 8
♣ 9 5

c
♠ J 9 2
♥ Q 8 3
♦ K Q 9 5 4
♣ 9 7

d
♠ 9 7 6 2
♥ Q 10 6 4
♦ 8 3
♣ K 9 5

3 Here it is your partner who has overcalled.

	LHO	*Partner*	*RHO*	*You*
	1♥	1♠	pass	?

a
♠ A 10 9 4
♥ 9 3
♦ K Q 10 6 3
♣ 7 5

b
♠ K J 5
♥ 7 6
♦ 10 9 8 5
♣ A K J 2

c
♠ 7 5 4
♥ A 6
♦ 10 8 6
♣ A Q J 7 3

d
♠ K Q 9 4
♥ A 8 5
♦ 2
♣ Q 10 8 7 2

ANSWERS

1 **a** 2NT   The diamonds are not strong enough for a fit-showing jump. You bid a Dormer (or Jordan) 2NT to show at least a limit raise but no strong side suit.

     b 3♣   Perfect for a fit-showing jump. You show a limit raise to 3♠ with a respectable side suit in clubs.

     c 4♦   You have the values for a raise to game that includes a side-suit singleton. Just right for a splinter bid of 4♦.

     d 3♦   You can make a fit-showing jump with three-card support, provided the trumps are headed by a top honor (ace, king or queen).

2 **a** 3♦   Perfect for a fit-showing jump response.

     b 3♣   A response of 2♠ would be natural and 3♠ would carry you past three of partner's suit (3♠ would be a splinter bid, in fact). So, your only option is a cuebid to show at least a limit raise of partner's suit.

     c 2♥   With three-card support and only 8 HCP, you are not strong enough for a fit-showing jump. If RHO had not overcalled, you would have raised only to 2♥.

     d 3♥   This raise is preemptive. With the same shape and limit raise values, you would cuebid 3♣ instead.

3 **a** 3♦   A textbook example of the fit-showing jump.

     b 2♥   You cannot make a fit-showing jump with only a four-card side suit. Cuebid instead, to show at least a limit raise.

     c 2♣   A fit-showing jump is not recommended when you hold only three small trumps. If you treat 2♣ as forcing here (not everyone does) you can start with that, intending to raise spades later; otherwise cuebid 2♥.

     d 4♦   Your club suit is not worthy of a fit-showing jump. Since you are strong enough to bid game, it is most accurate to make a splinter bid.

DOPI, ROPI and DEPO

W H A T ' S   I N   A   N A M E ?

 It's not clear who first came up with the idea of the DOPI convention. Certainly it's fairly recent: Easley Blackwood's own book, *Blackwood on Bidding*, published in 1956, discusses interference over Blackwood without mentioning DOPI at all.

In this chapter we will look at a group of conventions that are used rarely but are critically important when they do occur. Suppose your partner bids a Blackwood 4NT during a competitive auction and the next player bids 5♣. How do you let partner know how many aces (or keycards) you hold?

If your answer is: 'No idea. It doesn't happen very often!' you are in good company. Many players would have no idea what to do and that is one of the reasons why it is attractive to interfere over an opponent's 4NT enquiry.

Using the DOPI convention, you make use of Double and Pass when the opponents come in at the five-level over Blackwood. If you play traditional Blackwood responses, a Double shows no aces (or four, on rare occasions) and a Pass shows one ace.

These are the meanings of the various calls:

dbl	0 or 4 aces
pass	1 ace
1st available bid	2 aces
2nd available bid	3 aces

BY THE WAY

Since DOPI stands for:
Double = Zero, Pass = One
perhaps it should be written DOP1.

Here's a typical DOPI situation:

LHO	Partner	RHO	You
	1♠	pass	3♠
4♥	4NT	5♥	?

If you double now, you are showing zero or four aces, while pass would show exactly one ace. A bid of 5♠ would promise two aces, and 5NT three.

What if you play Roman Keycard?

Nowadays most players (in tournament bridge at any rate) use the greatly superior Roman Keycard Blackwood, which was described in *25 Bridge Conventions You Should Know*. When you use DOPI in conjunction with this version of Blackwood, this is what the responses mean:

dbl	0 or 3 keycards (aces and the trump king)
pass	1 or 4 keycards
1st available bid	2 keycards without the trump queen
2nd available bid	2 keycards with the trump queen.

Let's see some examples of this method in action.

♠ A J 6   ♥ K Q J 8 3   ♦ Q 10 2   ♣ 10 5

LHO	Partner	RHO	You
			1♥
3♣	4NT	5♣	?

Partner's 4NT agrees hearts as trumps and is Roman Keycard Blackwood. If RHO had passed, your response would have been 5♠ (two keycards, where the four aces and the trump king count as keycards, plus the trump queen). What should you bid now, playing DOPI responses over intervention? This is the meaning of each of the various calls here:

dbl	0 or 3 keycards
pass	1 or 4 keycards
5♦	2 keycards without the trump queen
5♥	2 keycards with the trump queen

The first available bid is 5♦. The second available bid is 5♥, so that is the one you must choose.

Playing Roman Keycard Blackwood, the 4NT bidder may follow up his initial inquiry with an inquiry about the queen of trumps. Let's look at an auction where this happens, despite enemy interference.

	Partner		You
	♠ A Q 9 8 2		♠ K 10 6 3
	♥ J 3		♥ A K Q 10 6 2
	♦ 10 2		♦ 9
	♣ K Q 10 5		♣ A 4

LHO	Partner	RHO	You
	1♠	3♦	4NT
5♦	pass	pass	5♥
pass	6♣	pass	6♠
all pass			

Partner's pass shows 1 or 4 keycards. You know there is an ace missing but decide you would still like to bid a small slam if partner holds the ♠Q. You make the first available non-trump bid (5♥ here) to ask if partner holds that card. Partner would sign off in 5♠ without the trump queen. Since he does hold the trump queen, he cuebids his lowest side-suit king. You were interested only in the trump queen on this occasion (the ♣K is a bonus). You bid the small slam, which is a near-certainty to make.

If partner had responded 5♠, over the 5♦ interference, this would have shown two keycards and the trump queen. You would then have bid 7♠.

BY THE WAY

Some players switch the meaning of Double and Pass and call the convention DIFS, to remind them that 'Double Is the First Step'. In other words, a double is equivalent to a normal 5♣ response which, in the 1430 response scheme, promises 1 or 4 keycards. A pass would show 3 or 0 keycards. There is no technical advantage to one method over the other.

Can't you just double them and take the money?

When partner's 'Pass' or 'Double' response tells you that there is no slam available your way, you can choose to take a penalty from the opponents' bid:

	Partner		**You**
	♠ Q J 4		♠ A K 5
	♥ A J 9 8 5 3		♥ K Q 6 4 2
	♦ K 5		♦ 4
	♣ 8 4		♣ K J 10 3

LHO	**Partner**	**RHO**	**You**
	1♥	3♦	4NT
5♦	pass	pass	?

You bid RKCB over the 3♦ intervention and LHO raises to 5♦, hoping that you and your partner will have no idea what to do next. Fortunately you were reading a great book on bidding only the previous evening and have agreed with your partner to play DOPI. Partner's pass shows 1 or 4 keycards.. Since you hold two keycards yourself, you know that partner must hold one rather than four here. Two aces are missing and you certainly don't want to be in 6♥. Since you are not certain to make even 5♥ (you will have to guess clubs if partner does not hold the ♣Q), the best idea is to double 5♦ and take whatever penalty you can against that contract.

What if you had bid 4NT on a hand with only one keycard and could not tell whether partner held one or four keycards? The bidding would go exactly the same way but partner would then bid on over your double if he held four keycards, knowing that at least a small slam was available your way.

Can you ask for side-suit kings after DOPI?

You can ask for side-suit kings in the usual way, by bidding 5NT. Various systems of responses are possible. The basic method described in *25 Bridge Conventions You Should Know* is that your partner tells you how many side-suit kings he holds (6♣=0, 6♦=1, 6♥=2, 6♠=3).

An alternative scheme is to cuebid your lowest side-suit king, if this can be done below six of the agreed trump suit. With no side-suit king, you will sign off in six of the agreed trump suit. This scheme can work well when you need to know which king partner holds. Look at this example:

	Partner		**You**
	♠ A Q 9 5 4 2		♠ K 10 8 3
	♥ A		♥ J 9 6 4
	♦ 4		♦ A 6
	♣ A Q J 10 2		♣ K 5 4

LHO	**Partner**	**RHO**	**You**
	1♠	pass	3♠ (limit)
4♦	4NT	5♦	5♥
pass	5NT	pass	6♣
pass	7NT	all pass	

Your 5♥ bid (the first available) shows two keycards without the trump queen. The 5NT continuation asks you to name your lowest side-suit king, if any. When you announce the king of clubs, it is easy for partner to bid 7NT. Had you shown the king of diamonds, or no side-suit king, partner would have stopped in 6♠. He would know then that there was a potential loser in the club suit.

Did you spot a problem with this scheme of responses? What should responder do when hearts are trumps and his side-suit king is in spades? He cannot show it without going past the safety level of six of the agreed trump suit. Responder should generally sign off in that case, unless he is sure that the spade king will be a valuable card. This would be the case, for example, if partner had bid the suit.

What if they bid higher than five of your suit?

Some opponents make life even more awkward over your 4NT, overcalling at the six-level (or at the five-level, beyond five of your trump suit). What then? It is not practical to play DOPI because some of the responses might take you too high. The professionals (and you, if you're taking the game seriously) have a counter available. It is known as DEPO, which stands for 'Double = Even, Pass = Odd'. The scale is condensed, because of the lack of available space:

dbl   0, 2 or 4 keycards (or aces, if you play simple Blackwood)

pass   1 or 3 keycards (or aces)

That's the basic scheme. In practice you are unlikely to double when you hold four keycards because you know then that a small slam (at least) will be playable. The same would be true if you unexpectedly held two aces when partner had announced a strong hand. In both those cases you should bid a small slam in the agreed trump suit. It is less of a problem to pass when you hold three keycards because if partner subsequently doubles, on the assumption that you hold only one keycard, you can still bid a small slam yourself. Partner will realize then that you have three keycards instead of one.

What if 4NT is doubled?

LHO	Partner	RHO	You
			1♥
3♦	4NT	dbl	?

This isn't an auction you'll encounter very often, but some nasty opponents like to throw in a double just to see whether you and your partner have discussed the situation!

One possibility is simply to ignore the double, of course, and make your usual Blackwood or RKCB response. However, you can save space by playing ROPI responses. You don't need to be a renowned psychic to work out that this stands for 'Redouble = 0 (or 3), Pass = 1 (or 4)'. It is exactly the same as DOPI except that Redouble takes the place of Double. The 5♣ and 5♦ responses show two keycards without and with the trump queen. This keeps you a level lower, and also gives you the option of playing in 4NT redoubled on some hands, if you want to.

Summary

✓ Playing DOPI after interference over RKCB, a double shows 0 or 3 keycards and a pass shows 1 or 4. The first available bid shows 2 keycards without the trump queen; the second shows two keycards with the trump queen.

✓ If you play traditional ace-asking Blackwood instead, a double shows zero or four aces and a pass shows one. The next two available bids show two and three aces respectively.

✓ Playing RKCB, the 4NT bidder may ask for the trump queen by making the next available non-trump-suit bid over partner's DOPI response.

✓ After interference at the six-level (or at the five-level beyond five of your trump suit), you can play DEPO. A double shows an even number of keycards (or aces) and a pass shows an odd number.

✓ After a double of 4NT you can play ROPI responses, where a redouble takes the place of the double in DOPI.

DOPI, ROPI AND DEPO

NOW TRY THESE...

1 Playing DOPI (and RKCB), what be your next bid in each case?

	LHO	Partner	RHO	You
				1♠
	3♥	4NT	5♥	?

a
♠ A Q J 9 6 3
♥ 7 2
♦ A 5
♣ J 9 3

b
♠ K J 9 8 2
♥ J 6 4
♦ A 10 8 3
♣ A

c
♠ Q 10 9 8 3 2
♥ K 9 6
♦ A K 7
♣ 3

d
♠ A Q 8 5 2
♥ K J 10 5
♦ K 2
♣ J 6

2 What will you bid next on each of these two hands?

	LHO	Partner	RHO	You
		1♠	3♣	4NT
	5♣	dbl	pass	?

a
♠ Q 10 7 6 2
♥ K Q J 7 3
♦ A K
♣ 3

b
♠ K Q 10 5
♥ A 9
♦ A K 10 9 6 2
♣ 4

3 Now the Unusual Notrump is used against you. What will you bid next in each case?

	LHO	Partner	RHO	You
		1♥	2NT	4NT
	5♦	pass	pass	?

a
♠ K Q 6 4 3
♥ A K 10 7 6
♦ A
♣ A 3

b
♠ A K Q 10 2
♥ K 6 5 2
♦ A J 9
♣ 4

4 Playing DEPO, what will you rebid on each of the following hands?

	LHO	Partner	RHO	You
				1♥
	3♣	4NT	6♣	?

a
♠ Q 8 7
♥ A K J 6 2
♦ A 9 3
♣ 10 7

b
♠ A Q 8 2
♥ A J 10 7 5 3
♦ 9 7
♣ 3

ANSWERS

1 a 5NT With two aces and the trump queen, you must make the second available bid.

b dbl A double shows 0 or 3 keycards. Partner will be able to work out, from the cards he holds, that you have 3 keycards.

c pass You have one keycard and must therefore pass.

d pass Again you hold only one keycard and must pass. You would no doubt like to double for penalties, with those great hearts, but you cannot do this when playing DOPI.

2 a 6♠ Partner has shown 0 or 3 keycards. It is very unlikely that he has an opening bid and no keycards, so assume he has three. In that case you are missing just one keycard and should bid the small slam.

b 5♠ Partner cannot hold three keycards, since there are only five and you hold three yourself. Strange as it seems, he must have no keycards and you should sign off. You could also decide to pass the double, of course.

3 a 7♥ Partner has one keycard, which must be the ♠A. Since he holds the values for an opening bid, it is a virtual certainty that he can make all thirteen tricks.

b 6♥ You are missing one keycard (almost certainly the ♣A). You would like to ask about the ♥Q but there is no space available. Bid 6♥ anyway. Partner is a big favorite to hold the trump queen. If not, he may hold six hearts or be able to finesse against the trump queen.

4 a pass You have an odd number of keycards (3) and should therefore pass over 6♣. If partner doubles at his next turn, you will bid 6♥ to show that you hold three keycards rather than one. Three is obviously enough for a small slam (at least).

b dbl With an even number of keycards (2), you double.

CHAPTER 16

PUPPET STAYMAN

WHAT'S IN A NAME?

Puppet Stayman was devised by California's **Kit Woolsey**. Woolsey, who has three medals in world competition to his credit, is the author of several excellent bridge books and is also a top-class backgammon player.

Suppose partner opens the bidding with 2NT, and you hold:

♠ J 9 2　♥ 9 5　♦ K 8 7 3　♣ J 6 4 2

You could simply raise to 3NT, but this may not be the best contract if partner happens to have a five-card spade suit. After all, it's quite normal to open 2NT on a hand with a five-card major (in fact, these days, it's quite normal to open 1NT with a five-card major). These could easily be the two hands:

Partner	*You*
♠ K Q 10 8 3	♠ J 9 2
♥ A 10 4	♥ 9 5
♦ A Q 6	♦ K 8 7 3
♣ A Q	♣ J 6 4 2

Now 4♠ is a great spot, while 3NT will be in serious jeopardy on a heart lead.

When you hold a five-card major opposite an opening notrump bid, it is easy enough to find a fit by using a Jacoby transfer. Similarly, it is straightforward to seek a 4-4 fit in a major, by using traditional Stayman. This is a different problem: how can you find a 5-3 fit in a major when, as responder, you hold a three-card major? The answer is to use Puppet Stayman.

What is Puppet Stayman?

For technical reasons this convention does not work particularly well opposite a 1NT opening. It is therefore mainly used when your partner has opened 2NT (or after the start of 2♣ - 2♦ ; 2NT). A 3♣ response asks opener about his major-suit holdings. Opener rebids as follows:

3♦	no five-card major, but at least one four-card major
3♥	five hearts
3♠	five spades
3NT	no four-card or five-card major

We will see in a minute that you will still be able to locate 4-4 fits in a major. Let's see how Puppet Stayman works on the example hand we started with:

Partner	You
♠ K Q 10 8 3	♠ J 9 2
♥ A 10 4	♥ 9 5
♦ A Q 6	♦ K 8 7 3
♣ A Q	♣ J 6 4 2
2NT	3♣
3♠	4♠

As we saw, 3NT would be at risk on a heart lead and you would rather play in the spade game. You respond 3♣, asking partner if he holds a five-card major. Partner's 3♠ response shows five spades and you raise to game in that suit. If partner had responded 3♦ instead, showing at least one four-card major but denying a five-card major, you would have bid game in notrump. If partner had rebid 3NT, denying even a four-card major, you would have passed.

The convention is particularly useful when responder has a singleton and is worried that this suit may be under-protected:

Partner	You
♠ K 8 3	♠ 2
♥ A Q J 7 3	♥ K 10 6
♦ A Q	♦ 10 8 7 3
♣ K J 5	♣ Q 10 6 4 3
2NT	3♣
3♥	4♥

3NT would not be a happy spot on a spade lead. You bid 3♣, seeking a 5-3 heart fit, and strike gold.

How do you locate a 4-4 fit?

The beauty of Puppet Stayman is that you can still find a 4-4 major-suit fit. When opener rebids 3♦, showing at least one four-card major, responder still has the necessary space to locate a 4-4 fit. How does he do this?

BY THE WAY

If you wish to use Puppet Stayman over partner's 1NT opening bid, you can do so most easily by bidding 3♣ over partner's 1NT. The responses and the rebids are the same as if partner had opened 2NT. Naturally, you will have to agree on this treatment.

After a start of 2NT - 3♣ ; 3♦ you might think that the simplest scheme for locating a 4-4 fit would be for responder to bid any four-card major that he held, seeking support. The problem with that method is that responder would often become the declarer. One of the reasons that transfer bids were invented was that it is desirable for the notrump opener to become declarer. The riches in his hand are then concealed from the defenders' view. The opening lead runs into the strong hand's tenaces, rather than through them.

So, on a similar principle to that of transfer bids, when responder has a four-card major he does not bid three of that suit: he bids three of the other major! With four hearts, for example, he will bid 3♠ at his second turn. If opener holds four hearts too, a 4-4 fit has been found. He will bid 4♥ and the strong hand will play the contract.

These, then, are your rebids:

Partner	You
2NT	3♣
3♦	?

3♥	shows a four-card spade suit
3♠	shows a four-card heart suit
4♦	shows four cards in both majors

It is these 3♥ and 3♠ bids that give the name 'Puppet' to the convention. Responder pulls the strings and partner can then bid the suit if there is a 4-4 fit.

Here is the Puppet part of the convention in action:

Partner	You
♠ K 4	♠ Q J 2
♥ A Q J 4	♥ K 10 6 3
♦ A J 9 3	♦ 6 5
♣ A Q 6	♣ 7 5 4 2
2NT	3♣
3♦	3♠
4♥	

Partner's 3♦ denies a five-card major but shows at least one four-card major. You then bid 3♠, showing a four-card heart suit. Since partner has four hearts too, he bids game in that suit and the club tenace is protected.

Let's see how the method works when you have two four-card majors:

Partner	You
♠ A J 3	♠ Q 10 9 4
♥ K Q 9 4	♥ A 10 6 3
♦ A K 3	♦ 6 5
♣ K 6 4	♣ 8 3 2
2NT	3♣
3♦	4♦
4♥	

Your 4♦ rebid shows four cards in both the majors. Partner bids 4♥ and becomes the declarer. Had you been the declarer, a lead though the ♣K might have spelled defeat.

In both the above examples, the contract would have been played by the wrong hand (the responder) if Puppet Stayman had not been available.

Summary

✓ A 2NT opening often contains a five-card major. When you hold a three-card major, as responder, you can use Puppet Stayman (a 3♣ response) to search for a 5-3 fit.

✓ After 2NT - 3♣ (Puppet Stayman), the opener rebids:

3♦	at least one four-card major
3♥	five hearts
3♠	five spades
3NT	no four-card or five-card major.

✓ After 2NT - 3♣ ; 3♦, responder may still seek a 4-4 fit in a major. Responder bids one major to show the other major (so that the 2NT opener can become declarer):

3♥	four-card spade suit
3♠	four-card heart suit
4♦	four hearts and four spades

PUPPET STAYMAN

NOW TRY THESE...

1 Playing Puppet Stayman, what would you bid over partner's opening 2NT on each of these hands? How will you proceed over his possible responses?

a	♠ A 9 6		**b**	♠ Q 6
	♥ 8 7			♥ K 10 9 6 4
	♦ K 10 8 5 3			♦ 8 7
	♣ J 7 2			♣ Q 9 7 3
c	♠ A 6		**d**	♠ A J 7 2
	♥ K J 8 7			♥ 9 8 3
	♦ 9 5 4 2			♦ J 5 2
	♣ 10 8 5			♣ 7 6 4

2 Playing Puppet Stayman, what would you rebid on each of these hands?

Partner	You
2NT	3♣
3♦	?

a	♠ A 2		**b**	♠ Q 10 9 5
	♥ K J 9 8			♥ J 7 6 4
	♦ 9 5 4			♦ 10 8 3
	♣ 10 6 3 2			♣ K 9

3 Now you are the 2NT opener. What will you bid next?

You	Partner
2NT	3♣
3♦	3♠
?	

a	♠ A Q 9 4		**b**	♠ K J 5
	♥ K 9 3			♥ A J 7 6
	♦ A K 10 3			♦ K 9
	♣ A 5			♣ A K J 9

ANSWERS

1 a 3♣   With a weak doubleton in hearts, you would like to play in a 5-3 spade fit if opener holds five spades. If partner rebids 3♦ or 3♥, you will sign off in 3NT. If he rebids 3NT, you will pass.

b 3♦   When you hold a five-card major yourself, you can use a Jacoby transfer.

c 3♣   To look for a 4-4 heart fit you will begin with Puppet Stayman. If partner rebids 3♦, denying a five-card major, you will continue with the Puppet bid of 3♠, showing your four-card heart suit.

d 3♣   Playing regular (four-card) Stayman, you would probably not bother looking for a 4-4 fit, dissuaded by the 4-3-3-3 shape. If you can find a 5-4 spade fit, via Puppet Stayman, that will be different. You would then be willing to play in 4♠.

2 a 3♠   Playing Puppet Stayman, you bid the major you do not hold. Here you rebid 3♠ and partner will then bid 4♥ if a 4-4 heart fit exists.

b 4♦   With both majors you rebid 4♦. Partner will then bid game in one of the majors (his 3♦ rebid guarantees a 4-4 fit somewhere).

3 a 3NT   Your partner has shown a four-card heart suit, remember. Since there is no 4-4 major-suit fit, you bid game in notrump.

b 4♥   With this hand you know you have a 4-4 heart fit.

SOPHISTICATED
STUFF

CHAPTER 17

INVERTED MINOR RAISES

WHAT'S IN A NAME?

 Inverted minor raises were part of the ***Kaplan-Sheinwold*** system developed in the early 1980s. The system included a weak 1NT opening and five-card majors, and was designed to give as many bids as possible precise definitions and limited strength ranges.

You are probably familiar with some conventional method for making a forcing raise of partner's major-suit opening. Depending on where you live, you probably play Jacoby 2NT, or Swiss, or some other similar convention. But what if partner's opening bid is in a minor suit? Suppose your partner opens 1♦ and you have to find a response on this hand:

♠ A 10 6   ♥ 6 2   ♦ A Q 10 6 4   ♣ A 9 5

Tricky, isn't it? A response of 3♦ would be a limit raise, promising 10-12 points. You can hardly make such a bid on this hand. What else can you try? 3NT is unappealing without a heart stopper – don't you just hate going down in 3NT when 5♦ or even 6♦ is cold? Nor is it attractive to jump straight to 5♦ when you have no idea how strong partner is. Playing standard methods, you would have to 'invent' a response such as 2♣ to find out more about partner's hand.

A useful convention is available to solve problems of this type. You reverse the meaning of the 2♦ and 3♦ responses (also of the 2♣ and 3♣ responses to 1♣), and make the 2♦ response forcing. The method is known as 'inverted minor raises'.

A raise of 1♣ to 3♣ (or 1♦ to 3♦) shows 6-9 points

A raise of 1♣ to 2♣ (or 1♦ to 2♦) is forcing and shows 10+ points

♠ A 10 6   ♥ 6 2   ♦ A Q 10 6 4   ♣ A 9 5

Partner	You
1♦	?

On the hand we saw before, you would respond 2♦, which is forcing and shows at least the values for a normal limit raise to the three-level. A 2♦ response is not exactly the same as a traditional 3♦ response because it is unlimited at the top end. If your system is such that partner may have a three-card suit for his opening bid in a minor, you promise at least five-card support for a raise.

Suppose you are weaker, with a normal two-level raise:

♠ 9 6   ♥ 10 7 4   ♦ Q J 6 4 3   ♣ K 9 2

Partner	You
1♦	?

Playing inverted raises, you respond 3♦ to show a hand in the 6-9 point range. You're worried about carrying the bidding so high with only 6 points? Don't be! The opponents surely have a good fit in at least one of the majors and your jump raise will make it more difficult for them to find it.

Note that when you give either a single or double raise of partner's minor you deny a four-card major.

♠ Q 8 6 4   ♥ 9 2   ♦ A J 7 5 2   ♣ 10 7

Partner	You
1♦	?

Partner opens 1♦ and you have splendid five-card support. It is tempting to raise preemptively to 3♦, aiming to shut the opponents out of the bidding. This tactic might work well but there is a danger that you would miss a 4-4 spade fit. It is better to respond 1♠, which may bring to light a fit in that suit.

What should you do with only four-card support?

In many systems, opening bids of 1♣ and 1♦ are sometimes made on a three-card suit. It is therefore risky to raise on four-card support and you should have five-card support. This is true, of course, even if you play your raises in the traditional manner with a double raise stronger than a single raise.

When you hold only four-card support for partner and have no suit to bid at the one-level, you can respond in notrump:

♠ Q 10 6　♥ 8 6 2　♦ J 10 6　♣ K Q 9 5

Partner	You
1♣	?

This shows a balanced hand of 6-10 HCP with no four-card major to bid.

Let's swap the minors on that hand:

♠ Q 10 6　♥ 8 6 2　♦ K Q 9 5　♣ J 10 6

Partner	You
1♦	?

When partner opens 1♦, you would again respond 1NT. However, you don't necessarily have four-card support for partner's suit in this auction. You might be 3-3-2-5 with five clubs, as on the following example:

♠ Q 10 6　♥ 8 6 2　♦ K 9　♣ Q J 10 6 5

Partner	You
1♦	1NT

A response of 2NT to a minor-suit opening is natural:

♠ K J 6　♥ Q 9 3　♦ J 9 7 3　♣ A J 4

Partner	You
1♦	?

If partner opens 1♦, you can respond 2NT, showing 11-12 HCP and no four-card major. Make the same response to an opening bid of 1♣. It is hardly worthwhile showing such a poor diamond suit.

How does the bidding go after 1♣ - 2♣ (or 1♦ - 2♦)?

The main objective of the partnership after a inverted minor single raise is to get to 3NT. It's a lot easier to make nine tricks than eleven. Of course, there will be hands where you will want to play in five (or even six) of your minor, but the initial assumption is that you are both looking to play in notrump.

Since responder has denied a four-card major when he raises a minor, any rebid by opener in a new suit shows a notrump stopper — not necessarily a four-card suit. Both players can then continue to show stoppers, which will help the partnership to judge whether 3NT is playable. Subsequent bids of 2NT or three of the opener's minor show that a player has nothing extra. They can be passed.

Let's see some typical auctions.

Partner	You
♠ 9 2	♠ K Q 4
♥ A K	♥ 5 3
♦ K J 9 7 6 3	♦ A Q 5 4 2
♣ A J 4	♣ 8 6 2
1♦	2♦
2♥	2♠
3NT	

Partner shows his heart stopper and you show your spade stopper. (If you held stoppers in both black suits you would bid 2NT or 3NT instead.) Partner has a secure stopper in clubs and 16 HCP, so he is happy to bid 3NT. The alternative game in diamonds would not be such a sound prospect.

On the next auction it becomes apparent that a suit is unprotected:

Partner	You
♠ A 2	♠ K 8 4
♥ 9 8 4	♥ 5 3
♦ A J 10 8 2	♦ K Q 7 6 3
♣ Q J 4	♣ K 7 6
1♦	2♦
2♠	3♦
pass	

Partner's 2♠ rebid shows a spade stopper but denies a heart stopper. (Otherwise he would have rebid 2♥; you always show your cheapest stopper.) Since you are weak in hearts too, you can guess that 3NT will not be a good idea. Your overall strength does not suggest that eleven tricks will be possible with diamonds as trumps, so you sign off in 3♦. If partner held extra values, he would make a further effort towards a diamond game himself. Note that since you know that the hearts are unstopped, there would not be much point in bidding 3♣ over 2♠, to show the club stopper.

Here you are stronger and have game in mind:

Partner	You
♠ K J 2	♠ 8 5
♥ 9 8 4	♥ A J 3
♦ A Q 10 8 2	♦ K J 9 7 4
♣ Q 4	♣ K J 6
1♦	2♦
2♠	3NT

Once you hear that partner has a spade stopper, you are happy to play in 3NT. Again it would be inappropriate for you to bid 3♣, showing the club stopper. Partner would then be entitled to think, 'I wonder why he didn't bid notrump.' He would conclude that you, too, must be weak in hearts.

Many players tend to overbid on opener's hand after a start of 1♣ - 2♣ (or 1♦ - 2♦). You often see players attempting 3NT with 13 points and then looking disappointed when partner puts down a dummy of 10 points, or even a shapely 9 points. Remember, he has not promised any more than that!

What happens if they overcall or double?

What about the situation when 1♣ or 1♦ is overcalled? Now responder has been presented with a new way to show a hand worth at least a limit raise: he can cue-bid the opponents' suit. Since you can't use a 1NT bid quite as freely now (it promises a stopper in their suit), the ranges also move down for the single and double minor-suit raises. This also lets you make it a little more difficult for the opponents when you have a good fit but a weak hand.

Here's an example of your options after a 1♦ opening and an overcall:

LHO	Partner	RHO	You
	1♦	1♠	?

With diamond support, you may choose from these bids:

2♦	shows 6-9 points
2♠	shows 10+ points
3♦	shows 2-5 points

Of course, you don't have to respond at the three-level whenever you hold the nominal requirements. Suppose you are vulnerable and hold this hand:

♠ 9 8 6   ♥ J 7   ♦ J 10 6 4 2   ♣ 7 5 2

LHO	Partner	RHO	You
	1♦	1♠	?

With this awful hand you would be understandably nervous of bidding 3♦, even if partner's opening bid has promised four diamonds. You might easily go for a penalty of 800 or so. You are perfectly entitled to pass when a raise greatly overstates the value of your hand.

With a better hand as responder:

♠ 9 6   ♥ 10 7 4   ♦ K J 6 4 3   ♣ Q J 9

LHO	Partner	RHO	You
	1♦	1♠	?

You raise to 2♦, showing 6-9 points. Make the clubs 9-x-x instead and you would raise to 3♦, indicating 2-5 points. Remember that bidding 3♦ here is a weak action indeed. You will see players rebidding 3NT on a balanced 18-count as opener, and looking somewhat puzzled when they go down.

It is more awkward when you have only four-card support:

♠ 8 5 3   ♥ 9 5   ♦ K 10 8 2   ♣ J 9 7 3

LHO	*Partner*	*RHO*	*You*
1♦	1♥	?	

Partner's 1♦ opening might be on a three-card suit. What do you say?

This represents a small downside for inverted raises. Playing traditional raises you might be willing to bid 2♦, not expecting this to be disastrous even if partner did happen to hold only three diamonds. Playing inverted minor raises, it is too risky to bid 3♦. You should pass.

When your partner's opening bid of 1♣ or 1♦ is doubled, you can bid 2NT to show at least a limit raise (10+ points). In that case, the single and double raises can have the same ranges as over an overcall.

Summary

✓ Playing 'inverted minor-suit raises', a single raise of a minor-suit opening (such as 1♣ - 2♣) is strong and forcing. It shows at least the values for a traditional limit raise (10+ points). A double raise (such as 1♣ - 3♣) is weak, showing 6-9 points. All raises of partner's minor-suit opening deny a four-card major.

✓ If partner's 1♣ or 1♦ opening may be based on a three-card suit, raises should contain five-card support. With only four-card support you will usually respond in notrump. A response of 2NT to one of a minor is natural, showing 11-12 HCP.

✓ After a start of 1♣ - 2♣, or 1♦ - 2♦, both players show stoppers in other suits for notrump purposes. Subsequent bids of 2NT or three of opener's minor may be passed.

✓ When 1♣ or 1♦ is doubled, or overcalled at the one-level, a single raise shows 6-9 points and a double raise shows 2-5 points.

✓ When 1♣ or 1♦ is doubled, you show a limit raise or better (10+ points) by bidding 2NT.

✓ When 1♣ or 1♦ is overcalled, you show a limit raise or better (10+ points) by cuebidding the opponent's suit.

INVERTED MINOR RAISES

NOW TRY THESE...

Playing inverted minor raises, what will you bid with each of these hands?

1
♠ A Q 2
♥ K 10 7
♦ K J 10 5 2
♣ 6 3

LHO	Partner	RHO	You
	1♦	pass	?

2
♠ 9 2
♥ 7 6
♦ J 9 8 2
♣ A J 8 4 3

LHO	Partner	RHO	You
	1♣	pass	?

3
♠ 2
♥ A 10 7 4
♦ K Q 9 6 2
♣ 9 8 3

LHO	Partner	RHO	You
	1♦	pass	?

4
♠ J 6
♥ A 10 7
♦ A K 10 5 3
♣ 7 6 2

LHO	Partner	RHO	You
	1♦	1♠	?

5
♠ A Q 8 6
♥ 4
♦ K J 5
♣ A J 10 8 7

LHO	Partner	RHO	You
			1♣
pass	2♣	pass	?

6
♠ Q J 6
♥ Q 10 4
♦ K 5
♣ K 10 9 8 2

LHO	Partner	RHO	You
	1♣	dbl	?

7
♠ A Q J 2
♥ 7 4
♦ A J 9 6 2
♣ 7 2

LHO	Partner	RHO	You
			1♦
pass	2♦	pass	2♠
pass	3♣	pass	?

8
♠ A K 10 2
♥ 8
♦ A K 10 9 8 3
♣ 9 2

LHO	Partner	RHO	You
			1♦
pass	2♦	pass	2♠
pass	3♣	pass	?

9
♠ 9 6 2
♥ A 10 7 4
♦ Q 9 8 5 3
♣ 7

LHO	Partner	RHO	You
	1♦	2♣	?

10
♠ J 6
♥ 8 3
♦ A J 10 5
♣ A Q J 8 7

LHO	Partner	RHO	You
	1♦	pass	?

ANSWERS

1   **2♦**   This is just the sort of hand where inverted raises are useful. Respond 2♦ and hope that partner can show a club stopper at some stage, allowing you to play in 3NT.

2   **3♣**   There is not much point in responding 1♦ on this hand. The opponents are likely to have a fit in at least one of the major suits and it is better tactically to bid 3♣. This shows a good club fit, 6-9 points, and no four-card major.

3   **1♥**   Remember that a raise of a minor-suit opening would deny a four-card major.

4   **2♠**   To show a limit raise or better of partner's suit you cuebid in the overcaller's suit. A response of 2♦ is still stronger than 3♦, even after interference, but now it shows only 6-9 points.

5   **2♦**   Your strongest stopper is in spades, yes, but at this stage you should bid the cheapest stopper. (A rebid of 2♠ would deny a stopper in either red suit.) If partner continues with 2♥, you will bid 3NT next. If partner denies a heart stopper, you can start thinking about playing in five or even six clubs.

6   **2NT**   Over a takeout double, you bid 2NT (Dormer) to show at least a limit raise of partner's suit.

7   **3♦**   It is likely that partner has a heart stopper because he has continued to show stoppers even though you denied a heart stopper yourself. Since partner chose not to bid notrump, he is probably quite strong and waiting to hear more about your hand. With a minimum, you sign off in 3♦.

8   **4♦**   Here your hand is more powerful and there is a good chance of a diamond slam. Indicate your extra strength with a jump to 4♦ or with a splinter jump to 4♥.

9   **2♦**   With 6-9 points, you make a single raise. It may look attractive to bid 3♦ but this would show only 2-5 points. You might then cause partner to misjudge the auction later.

10 **2♣**   With 13 HCP facing an opening bid there is no need to fear opposition bidding. Begin a description of your hand with a natural response of 2♣.

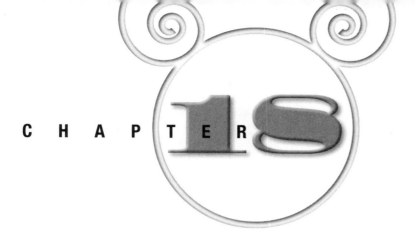

C H A P T E R **18**

LEAPING MICHAELS

W H A T ' S   I N   A   N A M E ?

 Michaels Cuebids were conceived by ***Mike Michaels*** *(1924-1966)*, a prominent writer and lecturer from Miami Beach, Florida. He was a close associate of the great Charles Goren, for whom he ghosted many nationally syndicated columns.

Basic Michaels Cuebids were described in a previous book in this series, *25 Bridge Conventions You Should Know*. They involve a simple overcall in the same suit that the other side has opened. For example, you might overcall 2♣ over 1♣. Such a cuebid promises a two-suited hand with at least 5-5 shape. This is the scheme:

Over 1♣	2♣ shows both major suits
Over 1♦	2♦ shows both major suits
Over 1♥	2♥ shows spades and an undisclosed minor
Over 1♠	2♠ shows hearts and an undisclosed minor.

When the responder to a major-suit Michaels Cuebid wants to know which minor the overcaller holds, he can bid 2NT. His partner will then bid 3♣ or 3♦ to show his minor suit.

BY THE WAY

Michaels Cuebids apply in the
fourth seat too, when the opening
bid is followed by two passes.

How strong a hand does a Michaels Cuebid show?

The most popular method is known as Mini-Maxi. The overcall is based on either a fairly weak hand or quite a strong hand. The ranges are about 6-10 points and 16+. When you are between these two ranges, you make a simple overcall in the higher of your suits instead, hoping to be able to bid the other suit on the next round. Responder assumes the weak type when calculating his response. Opener will bid again if he has the strong type.

In this chapter we will look at an extension of the method, one known as Leaping Michaels.

What is Leaping Michaels?

The Leaping Michaels convention may be used in two situations: when the opponents have opened with a weak two-bid, and when an opposing opening bid has received a single raise. Again it will show a two-suiter, at least 5-5.

Over an opening weak 2♦:

4♦   shows a two-suiter in spades and hearts

Over an opening weak 2♥:

4♣   shows a two-suiter in spades and clubs

4♦   shows a two-suiter in spades and diamonds

Over an opening weak 2♠:

4♣   shows a two-suiter in hearts and clubs

4♦   shows a two-suiter in hearts and diamonds

As you see, the two suits are identified immediately. The overall strength of the hand must be sufficient to justify bidding at such a high level.

Suppose RHO opens with a weak 2♦ and you hold:

♠ A J 10 8 3   ♥ K J 8 7 5 2   ♦ 4   ♣ A

LHO	Partner	RHO	You
		2♦	?

You would overcall 4♦, asking partner to choose a major at the four-level.

Let's consider a hand with less playing strength:

♠ K Q 9 8 2 ♥ A 9 7 6 2 ♦ 9 ♣ Q 3

LHO	**Partner**	**RHO**	**You**
		2♦	?

Here you cannot justify forcing partner to the four-level when there is no guarantee of a fit. You would have to overcall 2♠, possibly missing a fit in hearts if there was no further bidding.

Over a major-suit weak two, an overcall of 4♣ or 4♦ is not forcing but it does show considerable playing strength:

♠ 7 ♥ A Q 10 6 2 ♦ J ♣ K Q J 9 7 3

LHO	**Partner**	**RHO**	**You**
		2♠	?

BY THE WAY

It is in the nature of bridge players to extend conventions to new situations. You can also play Leaping Michaels when the opponents bid 1NT -pass- 2♥ (natural), or 1NT -pass- 2♦ (transfer). In these auctions, 4♣ would show spades and clubs, 4♦ would show spades and diamonds.

Here you would jump to 4♣, showing hearts and clubs. Partner is allowed to pass on a weak hand, when he prefers clubs.

You should not use Leaping Michaels on a major-minor hand when you hold a good six-card major, because there would be too much chance that a game in the major would be missed.

♠ — ♥ K Q 10 8 7 3 ♦ A K 9 4 2 ♣ 10 3

LHO	**Partner**	**RHO**	**You**
		2♠	?

Here you should bid 4♥, rather than 4♦ to show the two-suiter. Otherwise there is too much risk that partner will choose to play in diamonds when game in hearts is a good prospect.

The same convention may be used when an opponent's opening bid has attracted a single raise:

♠ K Q 10 9 5 ♥ 2 ♦ A Q J 8 4 2 ♣ 10

LHO	**Partner**	**RHO**	**You**
1♥	pass	2♥	?

You bid 4♦, showing a two-suiter in diamonds and spades.

♠ 5 ♥ Q 9 8 6 5 2 ♦ A ♣ K Q 10 8 4

LHO	**Partner**	**RHO**	**You**
1♠	pass	2♠	?

You can bid 4♣ on this hand to show hearts and clubs. (You are not worried about holding a six-card major here, because the hearts are so weak.)

With a major two-suiter you can use Leaping Michaels after a minor-suit raise auction by the opponents:

♠ K Q J 7 4 ♥ A J 10 8 5 2 ♦ A ♣ 6

LHO	Partner	RHO	You
1♣	pass	2♣	?

Whatever the strength of the 2♣ response, you jump to 4♣, showing a major two-suiter. You would also make the same 4♣ bid if RHO had raised to 3♣.

Can you use Michaels over a three-level preempt?

Some players use the same convention over a preempt at the three-level, when the bid made is not actually 'leaping' at all!

♠ 5 ♥ A Q J 8 3 ♦ A K J 8 2 ♣ Q 6

LHO	Partner	RHO	You
		3♠	?

Here they would bid 4♦, to show a two-suiter in diamonds and hearts. Of course, this agreement prevents you from making a natural 4♦ overcall. The need for such a bid is rare, though, since you will often be able to overcall 3NT when you hold good diamonds. (Many top players risk this even without a stopper in the opponent's suit! They hope that dummy will provide a stopper.) On frequency grounds it is more useful to play 4♣ and 4♦ overcalls as showing a two-suiter.

So what does a simple cuebid mean over a weak two?

Have you ever encountered a jump cuebid over an opening bid? These are most commonly used to show a solid minor suit and to ask partner to bid 3NT if he has a stopper in the enemy suit. Here's an example:

♠ 5 ♥ K 10 2 ♦ A 2 ♣ A K Q 10 8 4 2

LHO	Partner	RHO	You
		1♠	?

If your RHO opened 1♥ you would overcall 3NT, hoping that partner could stop the spade suit, or would have sufficient length there to prevent the opponents from cashing too many spade tricks. But what if RHO opened 1♠? Now the risk of several spade losers is considerable and you should overcall 3♠, meaning, 'Bid 3NT if you have a spade stopper, partner.' When your partner is not blessed with a spade stopper he will usually bid 4♣, looking to play in your long suit.

Playing Leaping Michaels, you don't need the cuebid to show a two-suiter over a weak two, so you can assign it the same meaning:

♠ 5   ♥ K 10 2   ♦ A 2   ♣ A K Q 10 8 4 2

LHO	Partner	RHO	You
		2♠	?

Bidding 3♠ here would ask partner to bid 3NT with a spade stopper.

✓ A Leaping Michaels overcall shows two specific suits. Over a weak 2♦ opening, an overcall of 4♦ shows both majors. Over a weak 2♥ or 2♠ opening, an overcall of 4♣ shows clubs and the other major, an overcall of 4♦ shows diamonds and the other major.

✓ When responder has a weak hand and better support for the minor suit, he may pass the 4♣ or 4♦ overcall.

✓ Leaping Michaels applies also when the opponents' auction starts with a one-level suit bid and a single raise.

✓ By agreement with your partner, you can play the same method over three-level preempts, when the bid will not be a jump. Over 3♦, for example, 4♦ would show the majors. Over three of a major, you would overcall 4♣ to show clubs and the other major, 4♦ to show diamonds and the other major.

✓ A direct cuebid over a weak two-bid (e.g. 3♦ over 2♦) can be used to ask for a notrump stopper.

LEAPING MICHAELS

NOW TRY THESE...

1 What would you bid on each of these hands when RHO opens a weak 2♥ and you are playing Leaping Michaels?

a	♠ A J 9 6 3	**b**	♠ A K J 7 6
	♥ 10 6		♥ 4
	♦ 7		♦ K Q 10 8 6 4
	♣ A K 8 7 2		♣ 9
c	♠ A K J 9 6 3	**d**	♠ J 10 8 6 5
	♥ 6		♥ —
	♦ K J 9 6 5		♦ A K 4
	♣ 4		♣ A K 8 7 4

2 On each of the following hands partner has overcalled a weak 2♠ with 4♣, Leaping Michaels. How will you respond?

a	♠ J 10 4	**b**	♠ Q 9 2
	♥ 9 8 2		♥ J 6
	♦ J 8 7		♦ Q 9 8 4 3 2
	♣ A 10 6 4		♣ 10 8
c	♠ 10 8 5 2	**d**	♠ 5
	♥ 9		♥ A J 5
	♦ A 8 4 3 2		♦ A 9 8 6 2
	♣ K 10 7		♣ K 8 7 3

3 The bidding starts

LHO	Partner	RHO	You
1♠	pass	2♠	?

Playing Leaping Michaels, what would you bid on each of these hands?

a	♠ 7 3	**b**	♠ J
	♥ A Q J 8 2		♥ A K J 7 5
	♦ —		♦ A K 10 9 4 2
	♣ A Q 10 9 6 4		♣ 4
c	♠ —	**d**	♠ A 9 2
	♥ A K J 10 7 4		♥ K 10 8 7 6
	♦ A 3		♦ —
	♣ J 8 6 5 2		♣ K 10 6 5 3

ANSWERS

1 **a** 2♠ You are not strong enough to force the bidding to the four-level. Make a simple two-level overcall.

  b 4♦ That's more like it! The 5-6 shape gives you more playing strength. Both suits have some solidity too.

  c 4♠ With such a strong six-card spade suit, you would be nervous asking partner to choose between spades and diamonds. How many spades should you bid? You are much too strong for 2♠ and partner might pass even a 3♠ overcall when holding enough for game. Go for all the marbles!

  d dbl The spades are weak and you have support for all three suits.

2 **a** 4♥ Even though you have better support for clubs, you should prefer the ten-trick game in hearts. Your support for hearts is perfectly adequate.

  b pass Your two queens are likely to be worthless to partner. Since he is more likely to hold six clubs than six hearts, you should choose to play in clubs even though this is not a game contract.

  c 5♣ With two useful cards you can raise to the minor-suit game with confidence.

  d 6♣ Here you have three splendid top honors and a possibly useful singleton in the enemy suit. Bidding cannot be particularly scientific in this situation but the chances of making a small slam are good.

3 **a** 4♣ Perfect for Leaping Michaels!

  b 4♦ Again, an ideal hand for the convention.

  c 4♥ With six good hearts you would be nervous about asking partner to choose between your two suits. Even if partner holds much better clubs than hearts, the two hands will play well in the heart game.

  d pass You would like to say something but you are not strong enough. If you double and partner responds in diamonds, which is very likely, you will be stuck.

CHAPTER 19

THE FORCING 1NT

WHAT'S IN A NAME?

 Facing an opening bid of 1♥ or 1♠, a Forcing 1NT Response is used in various bidding systems, such as *Two-over-One*, the *Precision Club*, *Eastern Scientific*, *Roth-Stone*, *Kaplan-Sheinwold*, and *Walsh*.

In most traditional bidding systems a 1NT response to one of a major is non-forcing and shows about 6-9 points. If you play a two-over-one system, where a two-level response such as 1♠ - 2♣ promises at least a good 12-count and is (usually) forcing to game, the traditional non-forcing 1NT response would leave you with no good response on a hand of 10, 11 or a bad 12 points. It is therefore an intrinsic part of two-over-one systems that after an opening bid of 1♥ or 1♠ a response of 1NT is forcing for one round. The response is used on various hands from 6 points up to a bad 12 points.

The Forcing 1NT response is also part of the Precision Club system, even though two-level responses are not forcing to game. The method is also favored by some players using Standard too, so it is well worth our having a look at it in this chapter. We will consider both its advantages and its disadvantages.

The principal disadvantage of the Forcing 1NT is that responder can no longer play in 1NT after his partner has opened 1♥ or 1♠. After a start such as 1♥ - 1NT, opener has to bid again and will often end up playing in two of his major on a 5-2 fit. Let's admit that this is a considerable drawback. If you play two-over-one, you have no choice but to play a forcing 1NT response, so you have to accept this negative feature. If you play Standard, you may well be unwilling to accept such a restriction. In that case you should continue to play a non-forcing 1NT with the traditional range of 6-9 points.

How does opener rebid after a forcing 1NT?

Much of the time opener's rebid will be obvious. If he has a second suit, lower than the first, he can show it with his rebid:

Partner	You
♠ K J 10 8 3	♠ 9 2
♥ A 4	♥ K Q 6 5
♦ A Q 7 2	♦ J 9 3
♣ 8 5	♣ Q 10 4 3
1♠	1NT
2♦	2♠
pass	

Partner has an obvious rebid in diamonds and passes when you give preference to the spade suit. You are quite likely to have only two spades for this sequence. With 6-9 points and three spades you would probably have raised to 2♠ directly.

Since opener has already shown a five-card suit by opening one of a major, he will normally have a six-card suit when he rebids his suit:

Partner	You
♠ A Q 9 7 6 3	♠ J 2
♥ 9 4	♥ K Q 6 5
♦ A 10 2	♦ J 9 3
♣ K 6	♣ A 10 7 2
1♠	1NT
2♠	3♠
4♠	

Partner rebids his six-card spade suit and you raise to the three-level, inviting game. Partner has just enough to accept the invitation.

Suppose partner had held the ♦K instead of the ♦10 on the last hand. He would then have rebid 3♠ instead of 2♠, to show a medium-strength hand with a six-card spade suit.

So far opener's rebid opposite a forcing 1NT has not caused a problem. Look at this hand, though:

♠ K Q 7 6 3　♥ A 10 5　♦ 9 4　♣ K 10 3

You	Partner
1♠	1NT
?	

What should you bid next? If 1NT were non-forcing you would happily pass. Here you do not want to rebid 2♠ because that would suggest a six-card suit. The best available rebid is 2♣, even though you have only three cards in the suit.

When you rebid in a minor, partner must allow for the fact that it may not be four cards long. For example, with a minimum responding hand containing two cards in your major and four cards in your minor, he will usually give preference to the major. That's what happens here:

You	Partner
♠ A J 8 5 2	♠ Q 7
♥ A 6	♥ K 10 8 2
♦ 9 8 2	♦ Q 10 3
♣ K Q 2	♣ J 7 6 3
1♠	1NT
2♣	2♠
pass	

If instead partner's shape were 1-4-4-4, with only one card in your major, he would have to pass the 2♣ rebid and hope that you held four clubs or that the 4-3 fit would be a reasonable spot.

An even trickier situation for opener arises on this type of hand:

♠ A Q 7 6　♥ A J 10 7 4　♦ Q 5　♣ 6 2

You open 1♥ and hear a forcing 1NT from across the table. What now? Partner has denied four spades and in any case you are not strong enough to reverse to 2♠. The choice lies between rebidding a two-card club suit (one that is only six-high!) and rebidding in hearts, pretending that you hold six cards in the suit. It is partly because of this problem that the Flannery 2♦ opening was invented, to cover minimum hands that are 4-5 in the major suits (see Chapter 2).

One positive feature of the Forcing 1NT is that it can allow you to play two of a minor on a weak hand, like this one:

	Partner	You
♠	10 8	J 7 2
♥	A K 7 6 2	8 3
♦	7 6 4	A 10 3
♣	A J 3	Q 8 6 5 2
	1♥	1NT
	2♣	pass

Partner rebids a three-card minor and you end up in a low-level eight-card fit. Playing Standard, the bidding goes 1♥ - 1NT, partner passes, and the final contract is unlikely to succeed.

What do you rebid, as opener, when you are strong with a fairly balanced hand?

♠ A K J 7 3   ♥ Q 10 5   ♦ A J 4   ♣ K 7

You	Partner
1♠	1NT
?	

You should rebid 2NT. This shows a hand of 5-3-3-2 shape and about 18 HCP. Perhaps you are thinking: why not 17 HCP? The answer is that with 15-17 HCP and a 5-3-3-2 shape you would have opened 1NT, even with a five-card major.

Suppose next that you have 5-4-2-2 shape with some strength to spare:

♠ A 9   ♥ K Q 10 9 5   ♦ K 4   ♣ K Q 7 4

You	Partner
1♥	1NT
2♣	2♥
?	

How many hearts is partner likely to hold? With three-card support he would usually have raised to 2♥ directly. He is much more likely to hold only two hearts. How many points will partner hold? Not enough to invite game himself, so he will be in the 6-10 point range. Since you hold 17 points yourself a game is still possible. You should suggest this by bidding 2NT at your third turn. Partner's main options will then be to pass, to sign off in 3♥ or 3♣ (since you did not rebid 2NT first time, he knows that you hold four clubs), or to raise to 3NT.

So why would you play a Forcing 1NT?

It is time to look at some of the advantages of playing a forcing 1NT response. The first is that you have a way to describe a weak hand that contains a long suit. Suppose partner opens 1♥ and you hold this hand:

♠ 7   ♥ J9   ♦ K Q 10 7 5 4 2   ♣ 9 6 2

Partner	You
1♥	?

You are not strong enough to respond 2♦. You bid 1NT (forcing) instead and wait to hear partner's rebid. Over a 2♣ rebid you will continue with 2♦. This shows a long diamond suit but a fairly weak hand, since you did not respond 2♦ initially. If instead partner rebids 2♥, you can bid 3♦ to convey the same meaning or you can decide to pass, since partner probably has six hearts.

Playing Standard, you still have to respond 1NT on this hand, since you are not strong enough to bid 2♦. If opener does not bid again, it's quite likely that you are not in the best contract.

Another advantage of playing the 1NT response as forcing is that you can use it to indicate different types of hand where you hold support for partner's major. When you have the values for a limit raise of the major (about 10-12 points), you have the choice between raising directly (1♠-3♠, for example) or bidding a forcing 1NT on the first round, followed by a bid of 3♠. You should choose this second route when you hold only three-card support:

♠ K 8 6   ♥ A 9   ♦ A 10 7 5   ♣ 10 9 6 2

Partner	You
1♠	1NT

If partner rebids 2♥, 2♦ or 2♣, you will bid 3♠ next. This is an invitation to game but warns partner that you hold only three-card support. If instead partner rebid 2♠, showing six spades, you raise all the way to 4♠.

Should you respond 1NT or two of a minor?

What should you respond to one of a major when you have a balanced hand of 11-12 points with a four-card minor?

♠ 8 6   ♥ A Q 9 3   ♦ K 10 7   ♣ Q 6 5 2

Partner	You
1♠	?

With 11 HCP it may seem okay to respond 2♣ playing Standard. Think again! What will you do next if partner rebids 2NT or raises you to 3♣? He may have 12 points, in which case you want to pass; he may have 14 points in which case 3NT may be a good spot. With no idea which, you will have to guess what to do next.

This would be an unwelcome situation, when playing Standard with a non-forcing 1NT response. The Forcing 1NT response comes to the rescue. You respond 1NT and, unless partner rebids 2♥, you will continue with 2NT to invite a game. Partner will decline when he has 12 points and accept when he has 14.

✓ If you play two-over-one, a two-level response is forcing to game and shows at least a good 12-count. You must therefore make use of a Forcing 1NT response to 1♥ or 1♠. Since this response guarantees another bid from the opener you can use it on various hand types, clarifying your strength on the next round.

✓ Even if you play Standard, where a two-level response shows only 10+ points, there are advantages in making the 1NT response forcing. The principal disadvantage is that a responder to 1♥ (or 1♠) can no longer play in 1NT. His partner will often have to play in 2♥ (or 2♠) on a 5-2 trump fit.

✓ With 6-9 points and a long suit you can respond 1NT with the intention of rebidding your suit on the next round. Partner will then know that you were not strong enough for an initial two-level response.

✓ When you have a limit raise of partner's major, and only three-card trump support, respond with a Forcing 1NT and then bid three of the major.

✓ Facing a Forcing 1NT response, the opener should rebid his major only with a six-card suit. With a shape such as 5332, he should rebid in his lower three-card suit.

THE FORCING 1NT

NOW TRY THESE...

1   On each of these hands, you are playing a Forcing 1NT response and part-
     ner opens 1♥. What is your response and what are your future plans?

a	♠ K 4	b	♠ K 8 4
	♥ 7		♥ J 6
	♦ A 10 9 8 7 3		♦ K 9
	♣ J 7 6 2		♣ Q 10 7 4 3 2

c	♠ A 10 6 2	d	♠ A 2
	♥ 7 4		♥ K J 8
	♦ K Q 7 4 3		♦ 9 7 6 2
	♣ 8 3		♣ K 10 7 6

e	♠ Q 10 6	f	♠ Q 2
	♥ A 4		♥ J 8
	♦ 10 9 6 5		♦ J 9 7 6 2
	♣ A J 8 3		♣ K 10 7 6

2   What rebid will you make on each of these hands?

	You	*Partner*
	1♥	1NT (forcing)
	?	

a	♠ Q 2	b	♠ Q 10 8 3
	♥ A K 9 8 4		♥ A K Q J 6
	♦ K 10 4		♦ 9 4
	♣ J 10 4		♣ 10 5

c	♠ 10 5	d	♠ K 10 2
	♥ A Q 10 8 6 4		♥ K Q 10 9 7
	♦ A		♦ A K 4
	♣ J 9 7 2		♣ K 6

e	♠ 6	f	♠ A Q J 2
	♥ A Q 9 8 2		♥ A K 10 7 6
	♦ A Q J 10 3		♦ 5
	♣ A 4		♣ K J 6

ANSWERS

1 **a** 1NT   If partner rebids 2♥, you will pass. If he rebids 2♣ (possibly on a three-card suit), you will rebid 2♦. If partner surprises you by rebidding 2♦, you are worth a raise to 3♦.

   b 1NT   If partner rebids 2♥, you will pass. If he rebids 2♦, you will correct to 2♥. A 5-2 fit in hearts will play well enough. Your clubs are not strong enough to rebid 3♣.

   c 1♠   A response of 1NT would deny a four-card spade suit.

   d 1NT   You have a limit raise in hearts (10-12 points) but only three-card support. Respond 1NT, intending to bid 3♥ on the next round.

   e 1NT   If partner rebids 2♦ or 2♣, possibly on a three-card suit, continue with 2NT. If instead partner rebids 2♥, showing six hearts, suggest game in that denomination by raising to 3♥.

   f 1NT   You intend to pass if partner rebids 2♥ or 2♦. If he rebids 2♣, you will correct to 2♥. You know there is a 5-2 fit in hearts and have no reason to expect that 2♦ will play better than 2♥.

2 **a** 2♣   A rebid of 2♥ would suggest a six-card suit, so you are forced to bid your lower three-card minor. Do not worry that the diamonds are stronger.

   b 2♥   Not a pleasant situation! You are not strong enough to 'reverse' to 2♠, which would carry the bidding too high when partner is weak. You must bid either 2♥, suggesting a six-card suit, or 2♣, suggesting at least a three-card suit. Here the hearts are excellent and it is better to pretend you have six hearts.

   c 2♥   Here you have a choice of two satisfactory rebids. Since the clubs are poor, it is better to emphasize the hearts. If instead your hearts were queen-high and the clubs were A-K-x-x, you would rebid 2♣.

   d 2NT   With a hand of this shape in the 12-14 range you would rebid 2♦, and with 15-17 you would have opened 1NT. Here you are strong enough to rebid 2NT, showing 18-19 HCP. If partner continues with 3♦ or 3♣, this will still be a sign-off on a weak hand, and you will pass.

   e 3♦   Again you are very strong and should rebid 3♦ rather than 2♦.

   f 2♠   Even though partner does not hold four spades, a 2♠ rebid is the best way of describing your shape and strength.

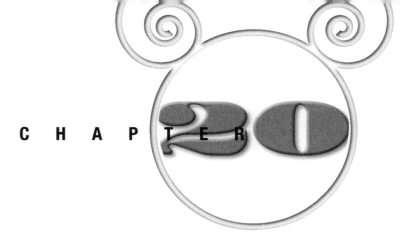

C H A P T E R **20**

ACE-AND-KING
(ITALIAN) CUEBIDDING

WHAT'S IN A NAME?

 It was the fabulous Italian Blue Team, spearheaded by *Giorgio Belladonna* and *Benito Garozzo*, who popularized the notion of treating aces and kings alike when cuebidding.

How do most players in the world bid a slam? After exchanging three or four bids, one player reckons there might be a slam. '4NT?' he says. Does this ask his partner's opinion about whether a slam may be possible? No! It says, 'Tell me how many aces (or keycards) you hold and I will make the decision.' In other words, the 4NT bidder has already decided to bid a slam unless two aces (or key-cards) are missing.

There is a much better way to approach slam bidding. You make a special type of bid (known as a cuebid) that suggests a slam to partner and invites his opinion on the matter. If he likes the idea of a slam, he can make a similar bid himself or perhaps bid Blackwood. If he does not like the idea, because his hand is unsuitable for a slam, he can sign off. Partner's bid of 4♣, in the following auction, is an example of a cuebid:

> **BY THE WAY**
>
> *The term 'cuebid' is also used in a completely different context. It can mean a bid made in the opponent's suit, usually to indicate strength.*

	You	Partner
	1♦	1♠
	3♠	4♣

Spades have been agreed as trumps and partner's bid in a new suit (usually at the four-level or higher) is a cuebid. It suggests a slam in spades and shows a control in the club suit. The previous book in this series, *25 Bridge Conventions You Should Know*, introduced the idea of a cuebid. It described the standard method where, unless your hand is known to be very weak, your first cuebid in a suit shows that you have first-round control in that suit, i.e. the ace or a void.

In this chapter we will look at an alternative method, known as 'ace-and-king cuebidding' or 'Italian cuebidding'. It is widely favored by expert players and is, in many ways, easier to use. At the end of the chapter you will be able to make up your own mind which method of cuebidding you prefer.

Before describing this particular style of cuebidding, let's have a brief refresher on how you can tell if a bid is a cuebid.

When is a bid in a new suit a cuebid?

What is the general rule for recognizing that a bid is a cuebid?

> *Once a trump suit has been agreed, and the bidding is forced to the game level, a bid of a new suit (usually at the four-level or higher) is a cuebid.*

Look again at the example we gave above:

	You	Partner
	1♦	1♠
	3♠	4♣

BY THE WAY

Some writers on the game are trying to rename (control-showing) 'cuebids' as 'control bids'. Old habits die hard, however, and it will be many years — if ever — before players are willing to drop the name 'cuebid' in this context.

A trump suit has been agreed (spades). Partner's 4♣ is a bid in a new suit at the four-level, so it is a cuebid. Its full title is a 'control-showing cuebid'.

Sometimes you agree a suit at the two-level; you may wonder why a bid in a new suit is not then also a cuebid. Look at this familiar auction:

	Partner	You
	1♠	2♠
	3♦	

Partner's 3♦ is not a cuebid, because the bidding is not yet forced to the game level. It is a 'game try', perhaps a help-suit game try as explained in *25 Bridge Conventions You Should Know*. If so, it asks you to judge whether to bid 3♠ or 4♠, based on whether your diamond holding will help to eliminate the announced losers in partner's diamond suit. A short diamond holding (two or fewer) would be helpful, for example, because partner could then ruff one or more diamonds in dummy.

When a minor suit has been agreed at the two- or three-level, any bids in a new suit that are below the level of 3NT will be aimed at discovering whether a notrump game is possible. Look at this auction:

Partner	You
1♠	2♣
3♣	3♦

Clubs have been agreed as trumps but since you need eleven tricks to make a game in clubs, it is attractive to investigate whether 3NT is playable. Your bid of 3♦ is not a cuebid. It shows a diamond stopper and invites partner to rebid 3NT if he holds a heart stopper.

We said that cuebids are usually at the four-level or higher. One exception arises on auctions of this type:

You	Partner
1♦	1♥
3♥	3♠

Hearts have been agreed as trumps and, once partner bids again, the auction is forced to the game-level at least. So, partner's 3♠ is a cuebid inviting a slam.

(You cannot cuebid in the trump suit itself, of course. When a player bids the next level of the trump suit, this is a sign-off, indicating that he can see no reason for going any higher.)

Can you imply that trumps are agreed?

You are itching (or perhaps somewhat nervous!) to hear about ace-and-king cuebids. We realize that, but there is one other important piece of background knowledge to remind you about. In the cuebidding auctions that we have seen so far, a trump suit was explicitly agreed. What does that mean? It means that both partners made a bid in the intended trump suit. In the last auction in the previous section, for example, both players made a bid in hearts and that suit was therefore explicitly agreed as trumps. Sometimes, though, it is the cuebid itself that agrees a trump suit. Look at this start to an auction:

You	Partner
1NT	3♠
4♦	

Partner shows at least six spades and suggests a spade slam. If you do not like the idea of a slam for some reason, you can bid either 3NT or 4♠. Your actual bid of 4♦ is a cuebid that agrees spades as trumps. Spades have not been explicitly agreed but your 4♦ bid performs two roles: it agrees spades as trumps and shows a diamond control.

Let's see another auction where it is sensible to play that the last-shown bid is a cuebid that agrees partner's suit as trumps.

You	Partner
1♥	2♠ (strong)
3♥	4♦

Partner's 4♦ is a cuebid showing a diamond control and agreeing hearts as trumps. Partner would not have made a jump shift on a two-suited hand. If he just held a long and strong spade suit he would rebid 3♠. His actual rebid of 4♦ shows that he made the jump shift because he held excellent hearts as well as spades.

What are the advantages of ace-and-king cuebidding?

At the start of the chapter we mentioned that the basic method is that the first cuebid in a suit promises the ace of that suit. It is a playable method but we are now (at last!) going to look at ace-and-king (Italian) cuebidding, where a cuebid shows either the ace or the king of the suit bid. Why should you want to follow this style?

The first advantage is that when partner does not cuebid in a suit you know he holds neither the ace or king. If you yourself hold neither of those cards, you can tell that the suit is uncontrolled. The opponents can cash the ace and king there and no slam will be possible. Look at this auction, using ace-and-king cuebidding:

You	Partner
♠ K Q 7 3	♠ A J 10 9 6 2
♥ A Q J 10 2	♥ K 6
♦ 2	♦ A 8
♣ Q 5 4	♣ J 10 7
1♥	1♠
3♠	4♦
4♠	pass

Your 3♠ bid agrees spades as trumps and partner's 4♦ is a bid in a new suit at the four-level. So, it is a cuebid! What does it mean? Partner's 4♦ passes these three messages:

(a)   'I am interested in a spade slam.'

(b)   'I have the ace or king of diamonds.'

(c)   'I do not have the ace or king of clubs.'

Why does partner deny the ace or king of clubs? Because, holding one of those cards, he would have cuebid 4♣ instead. You always cuebid your cheapest control. Since you have no club control yourself, you know that the defenders can cash the ace and king of clubs! You sign off in the safe contract of 4♠.

Suppose your bidding system permits you to cuebid only when you hold an ace. Again partner would cuebid 4♦ but this time you would have no idea whether partner held the king of clubs. You might decide to continue with a cuebid of 4♥. Partner would then have no idea whether you held a club control. From his point of view, as indeed is the case, you may be continuing to cuebid in the hope that he holds the king of clubs.

This is the first advantage of ace-and-king cuebidding, then. You can discover when there is no control in one of the side suits.

When one player has denied any control in a suit, a subsequent cuebid from his partner in a different suit carries a special implication. What do you make of this start to an auction:

You	Partner
1NT	3♠
4♦	4♥

Partner's 3♠ bid shows at least six spades and invites a slam. Your 4♦ bid is a cuebid that passes these messages:

(a)   'Yes, I have a spade fit and like the idea of a slam.'

(b)   'I have the ace or king of diamonds.'

(c)   'I do not have the ace or king of clubs.'

Nothing difficult there, but what messages does partner's 4♥ convey? It shows a heart control, yes, but do you see why it also shows a club control? You have denied a club control (ace or king), so unless partner had a control in that suit he would sign off in 4♠, knowing that there were two top club losers. Make sure you have understood this before reading on. It is an important aspect of ace-and-king cuebidding.

The next big advantage of cuebidding kings as well as aces is that a player can identify a particular king. That's what happens here:

You	Partner
♠ A K Q 10 9 7 2	♠ J 6 4
♥ 5	♥ J 10 8 3
♦ A Q 8 5	♦ K 7 2
♣ A	♣ J 10 7
2♣	2♦
2♠	3♠
4♣	4♦
4NT	5♦ (0 keycards)
6♠	

You open 2♣ and the spade fit comes to light. You continue with a cuebid of 4♣ and partner is able to cooperate with a cuebid of 4♦ on the king. Eureka!

The king of diamonds is just the card that you wanted to hear about. You use Roman Keycard Blackwood, just in case partner also holds the ♥A. When that card is missing you content yourself with a small slam.

Suppose that you were restricted to cuebidding only when you held an ace. Partner would not be able to show the ♦K and the slam would be missed. You can hardly afford to carry the bidding to the five-level, searching for the missing king. If partner did not hold the ♦K, the five-level might prove to be too high.

How do you distinguish between the ace and the king?

Perhaps you are worried that you will run into some problems caused by not knowing if partner holds the ace or the king in a suit that he has cuebid. Often this will not make any difference. If you hold the ace or king yourself, you will know that partner is cuebidding the king or ace, respectively. Similarly, if you hold Q-x in a suit that partner has cuebid, you will expect to lose one trick there whether he has the ace or the king.

In cases where it does matter which of the two cards he holds — opposite a singleton in your own hand, for example — you can resolve the problem by using Blackwood after an exchange of cuebids. That's what happens here:

You	Partner
♠ A K Q 7 3 2	♠ J 9 6 5
♥ 2	♥ A 7 6 4
♦ A Q 9 7	♦ 10 6
♣ A K	♣ 10 8 5
2♣	2♦
2♠	3♠
4♣	4♥
4NT	5♣
6♠	

Partner's 4♥ is an ace-or-king cuebid. Since he did not make the cheaper cuebid of 4♦, he denies the ace or king of that suit. You do not know partner's precise diamond holding but it is reasonable to hope there will not be two losers in the suit, given your own holding. You therefore decide that you wants to bid 6♠ if partner has the ♥A but not if he has the ♥K. Your next bid is 4NT, to ask partner how many keycards he has. Partner's 5♣ shows one keycard (playing 1430 responses) and you bid the slam. If partner had denied any keycards, his heart cuebid having been made on the king, you would have signed off in 5♠.

Here is another auction. This time you are interested in a grand slam.

You	Partner
♠ A 10 7 3	♠ K Q 6 4 2
♥ A Q 6 4 3 2	♥ K 7
♦ A 5	♦ 10 8 6
♣ 2	♣ A J 7
1♥	1♠
3♠	4♣
4♦	4♥
4NT	5♠
7♠	

You agree spades as trumps and three cuebids follow. Once again you can see how valuable it is for partner to be able to show a specific king. The ♥K is priceless, so far as you are concerned. Although you have heard a cuebid in clubs, you need to know, on this hand, whether partner holds the ♣A or the ♣K. Roman Keycard Blackwood provides the answer. Partner shows that he has two keycards (the ♠K and ♣A) plus the ♠Q. You now bid the grand slam, realizing that you may need to find some reasonable breaks if partner has only four spades. Fortune favors the brave and on this occasion partner holds five trumps, making the grand slam a superb contract.

It would be foolish of us to pretend that slam bidding is a precise art. Even experts find it very difficult and often get to the wrong contract. You can see, though, how cuebids (in particular ace-and-king cuebids) can help you to bid more accurately.

What about singletons or voids?

Once you have become accustomed to ace-and-king cuebidding, you may feel able to take one further step into the great unknown! Sometimes, particularly when you are the player with the shorter trump holding, you will feel able to make a cuebid not on an ace or king, but on a void or singleton. A shortage can be just as effective as an ace or king in preventing the defenders from cashing two tricks against a slam.

Here is an auction where partner feels he is entitled to cuebid a singleton:

You	Partner
♠ A K J 10 7 6 2	♠ Q 8 5 3
♥ A J 6	♥ 7
♦ K	♦ Q 10 7 6
♣ A K	♣ J 9 8 5
2♣	2♦
2♠	3♠
4♣	4♥
6♠	

Partner agrees spades as trumps and you suggest a slam with a cuebid of 4♣. Partner can see that his singleton heart will be nearly as useful as a king. It will allow you to score extra tricks by ruffing any losing hearts. Rather than sign off in 4♠, he cuebids his heart control. This is just what you wanted to hear! You leap to 6♠, hoping to lose one diamond trick and nothing more.

You'd like to be able to bid slams like this... don't deny it! It is only possible if you are willing to take a more flexible attitude towards cuebids and show both first- and second-round controls.

Summary

✓ When a trump suit has been agreed and the partnership is committed to game, a bid in a new suit, usually at the four-level or higher, is a cuebid. It suggests a slam and shows the ace or king in the suit bid.

✓ One advantage of this method is that you can detect when you are missing the two top cards in a side suit and will therefore not be able to make a slam.

✓ Another advantage is that you can show a specific king, which may fit well with partner's holding (A-Q-x-x, for example, or A-x).

✓ On hands where you need to know whether partner's cuebid is based on the ace, rather than the king, you can use RKCB after exchanging cuebids.

ACE-AND-KING (ITALIAN) CUEBIDDING

NOW TRY THESE...

1   Is the last bid in each of these incomplete auctions a cuebid or not?

a
Partner	*You*
1♣	3♣ (10-12)
3♦	

b
Partner	*You*
1♠	2♦
2♥	3♥
4♣	

c
You	*Partner.*
1♠	1NT
4♠	5♣

d
You	*Partner*
1♠	1NT
3♥	4♦

2   Playing ace-and-king cuebidding, what should you bid next on each of these hands?

a   ♠ J 10 4
♥ A Q J 7 2
♦ Q 8
♣ A K 6

Partner	*You*
1♠	2♥
3♠	4♣
4♥	?

b   ♠ 9 2
♥ A Q 9 3
♦ A 8 4
♣ J 10 8 2

Partner	*You*
1♥	3♥ (10-12)
3♠	?

c   ♠ Q 10 8 5 2
♥ Q J 4
♦ 8
♣ K 10 7 2

Partner	*You*
1♠	4♠
5♣	?

d   ♠ A 5 4
♥ K 5
♦ A J 8 6
♣ K Q 7 3

Partner	*You*
	1NT (15-17)
3♠	?

e   ♠ Q 3
♥ A Q J 8 2
♦ K 4
♣ A 10 9 6

Partner	*You*
	1♥
3♥ (10-12)	?

f   ♠ A Q 8 7 6
♥ K Q J 6 5
♦ A 9
♣ 4

Partner	*You*
1♦	1♠
3♠	?

ANSWERS

1   **a**   No   3♦ shows a stopper bid, aiming for a notrump contract. Your side is not yet committed to game. When a minor suit has been agreed, all bids in a new suit below 3NT show stoppers

       b   Yes   Hearts have been agreed as trumps and 4♣ is a bid in a new suit at the four-level.

       c   Yes   It would make no sense for partner to suggest clubs as a trump suit. He obviously has a very useful hand if spades are trumps and is showing a club control.

       d   Yes   Partner's 4♦ shows a diamond control and a hand that contains exceptional support for hearts. (If he held exceptional support for spades he would not have responded 1NT.)

2   **a**   4♠   Partner has denied a diamond control, so you should sign off in 4♠.

       b   4♦   Partner's 3♠ suggests a heart slam. With two aces, you are more than happy to cooperate, so you make a cuebid in diamonds. At the same, time, you're letting partner know about the potential problem in clubs – if he makes another move, then he has clubs covered himself.

       c   5♦   With five-card trump support your singleton diamond is at least as valuable as the ♦K. Partner will be able to ruff all his losing diamonds. (You were not quite worth a splinter bid of 4♦ on the first round.)

       d   4♣   Partner has six spades and is suggesting a spade slam. You have good spade support and plenty of controls. Accept his offer by cuebidding your cheapest ace or king.

       e   4♥   You are not quite strong enough to suggest a slam on this auction. You should simply raise to game.

       f   4NT   There is no need to make a cuebid on this hand. You have first- or second-round control in every suit and you are strong enough to bid Roman Keycard Blackwood immediately.

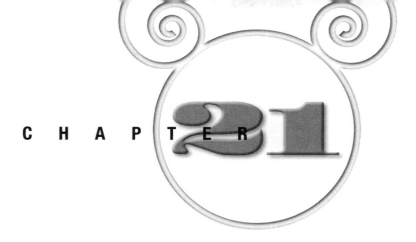

CHAPTER 21

UNUSUAL OVER UNUSUAL

 WHAT'S IN A NAME?

This convention was among a number of bidding ideas first proposed by **Monroe Ingberman**, of White Plains, NY. You might be interested to check out some of his other creations: 3NT as a forcing major raise and Fragment Bids are two conventions that are still quite popular.

Suppose your partner opens 1♥ or 1♠ and the next player overcalls 2NT — the Unusual Notrump, showing both minor suits.

LHO	Partner	RHO	You
	1♠	2NT	?

Suddenly, your carefully worked-out system of spade raises goes out of the window, as a whole level of bidding space has disappeared. So what will you bid on each of the following possible hands?

♠ Q 9 7   ♥ Q 10 5 3   ♦ K 8 3 2   ♣ 10 7

On this one, you would have bid 2♠.

♠ A 10 7 3   ♥ K 8 7   ♦ 9 2   ♣ K 9 8 2

This hand would have been worth a limit raise to 3♠.

♠ A 10 7 3 ♥ K 8 7 ♦ A 2 ♣ K 9 8 2

This one is worth a game raise, via Jacoby 2NT, or whatever you use.

Your opponent, as he intended, has created a problem for you. However, as we will see, by effectively bidding both clubs and diamonds, he has also added two extra cuebids to your arsenal. The question is how best to employ them.

What should the cuebids mean?

LHO	Partner	RHO	You
	1♠	2NT	?

Suppose you bid 3♣ or 3♦ now. These bids are obviously not natural, after an opponent has indicated at least five cards in each of these suits. What should they mean? The overcall has left you with very little space to describe your hand as responder, and it is essential that you make good use of the two cheap bids in the enemy suits. Various methods are in use, but this is one of the most popular:

3♣	at least five hearts (10+ points)
3♦	limit raise or better in spades (10+ points)
3♥	a good six-card heart suit (6-9 points)
3♠	normal raise to 2♠ (6-9 points).

The scheme is similar when partner opens 1♥:

LHO	Partner	RHO	You
	1♥	2NT	?

3♣	limit raise or better in hearts (10+ points)
3♦	at least five spades (10+ points)
3♥	normal raise to 2♥ (6-9 points)
3♠	a good six-card spade suit (6-9 points).

How do you remember this? All club bids are linked to hearts; all diamond bids are linked to spades. A bid at the three-level in partner's suit shows that you would normally have raised to the two-level (it is very important not to be shut out on such hands). A bid in the other major is non-forcing and shows the equivalent of a weak two-bid opening in that suit.

Let's see how you would bid the example hands from before, using this method:

♠ Q 9 7   ♥ Q 10 5 3   ♦ K 8 3 2   ♣ 10 7

LHO	Partner	RHO	You
	1♠	2NT	?

LHO	Partner	RHO	You
	1♥	2NT	4♦

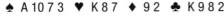

agrees hearts and shows a singleton or void in diamonds.

You respond 3♠, telling partner that you are worth only a raise to 2♠. There are two worthwhile benefits of this action. First, your partner will be glad to hear the response when he has 18 or 19 points and can bid game in spades. Second, you prevent the fourth player from saying, at a cheap level, which minor he prefers.

Suppose you are slightly stronger:

♠ A 10 7 3   ♥ K 8 7   ♦ 9 2   ♣ K 9 8 2

LHO	Partner	RHO	You
	1♠	2NT	?

Now you are worth a limit spade raise to the three-level. Should you respond 3♠? No, because this response shows a weak hand, as we have just seen. Instead you bid 3♦ (diamonds are linked to spades, remember, so this shows a spade raise). Partner can now sign off in 3♠ when he has a minimum-range hand or head for game or a slam when he is stronger.

♠ A 10 7 3   ♥ K 8 7   ♦ A 2   ♣ K 9 8 2

LHO	Partner	RHO	You
	1♠	2NT	?

Finally, even on this stronger hand, you still start with a bid of 3♦. Remember, this shows *at least* a limit raise in spades. If partner signs off in 3♠, you will bid game anyway.

Now let's look at some hands where you hold the other major suit, hearts.

♠ 10 3   ♥ A Q 10 5 3 2   ♦ J 5   ♣ A 7 6

LHO	Partner	RHO	You
	1♠	2NT	?

With 10+ points and a heart suit you bid 3♣ (clubs are linked to hearts). If partner has 15 points or more, he must make a rebid other than 3♥ or 3♠, which you can pass.

When you have a weak two-bid type hand in hearts, you bid 3♥ directly:

♠ J 5   ♥ K Q 10 6 4 3   ♦ Q 9 2   ♣ 8 5

LHO	Partner	RHO	You
	1♠	2NT	?

Your response of 3♥ is non-forcing and describes your hand well. Your

UNUSUAL OVER UNUSUAL

partner can decide whether to pass or make another bid. You should use these 6-9 point non-forcing bids only when you have a good suit. That's especially true when partner has opened in hearts and you hold six spades. You cannot afford to bid 1♥ - (2NT) - 3♠ unless your spade suit is strong enough to play at this level.

How does the auction continue?

There are no particular problems in continuing the auction. Because you are making good use of all four three-level suit bids, partner will have a good picture of your hand and can bid accordingly. Let's look at some typical auctions:

	Partner		You
	♠ 5		♠ K Q J 5 4 2
	♥ A Q J 8 6		♥ 9 5
	♦ A 10 4 3		♦ 9 6
	♣ K 5 2		♣ J 8 3

LHO	Partner	RHO	You
	1♥	2NT	3♠
all pass			

Partner does not like spades as a trump suit but must pass and hope for the best. With only 6-9 points opposite, it is clear to him that the values for 3NT are not present.

	Partner		You
	♠ J 7 6		♠ K Q 10 5 4
	♥ A J 10 6 2		♥ 9 5
	♦ A Q 3		♦ J 9 3
	♣ 9 2		♣ A 6 5

LHO	Partner	RHO	You
	1♥	2NT	3♦
pass	3♠	all pass	

Here you show 10+ points with at least five spades (diamonds are linked to spades). Partner has a minimum hand with spade support and bids just 3♠, which ends the auction. With a couple of points more, he would have rebid 4♠ instead.

What does a double of 2NT mean?

One other call at your disposal over the 2NT overcall, of course, is 'double'. What is this used for?

LHO	Partner	RHO	You
	1♠	2NT	dbl

The double of an Unusual 2NT overcall is used to show that you are interested in making a penalty double of three of a minor. Almost always you will have fewer than three cards in support of partner's major. Otherwise you could probably score better by playing a contract in your own direction.

Suppose neither side is vulnerable:

♠ 8 3   ♥ A 10 9 4 3   ♦ A Q 9 5   ♣ J 7

LHO	Partner	RHO	You
	1♠	2NT	?

You are happy to double. You have excellent defense against diamonds yourself. If LHO bids 3♣ over your double, your partner may be able to double.

Now give yourself some spade support:

♠ K Q 6   ♥ K J 10 5   ♦ A 10 2   ♣ 9 8 4

LHO	Partner	RHO	You
	1♠	2NT	?

The prospects for a double are not so good on this hand. Why is that? Your five points in spades will be wasted on defense when the 2NT bidder holds a singleton spade. Meanwhile you are a big favorite to score a game your way in spades or notrump. Respond 3♦, to show spade support and 10+ points. Even if partner signs off in 3♠, you will go on to game.

✓ When partner's 1♥ opening is overcalled with an Unusual 2NT, you may make these responses:

3♣	at least a limit raise in hearts (10+ points)
3♦	at least five spades (10+ points)
3♥	a normal raise to 2♥ (6-9 points)
3♠	a good six-card spade suit (6-9 points)

✓ When partner's 1♠ opening is overcalled with an Unusual 2NT, you may make these responses:

3♣	at least five hearts (10+ points)
3♦	at least a limit raise in spades (10+ points)
3♥	a good six-card heart suit (6-9 points)
3♠	a normal raise to 2♠ (6-9 points)

✓ A double of 2NT shows interest in penalizing the opponents. Opener is encouraged to double any bid of three of a minor.

UNUSUAL OVER UNUSUAL

NOW TRY THESE...

1 Playing Unusual over Unusual, what would you bid with each of these hands?

	LHO	*Partner*	*RHO*	*You*
		1♥	2NT	?

a ♠ A Q 10 9 6 3
♥ 7
♦ 6 5
♣ 10 9 7 3

b ♠ A J 9 8 2
♥ J 6 4 3
♦ 8 3
♣ 9 5

c ♠ A K 10 2
♥ K 9 6 5
♦ Q 7 3
♣ 3 2

d ♠ A K J 7 2
♥ 9 3
♦ A 10 7 4
♣ 6 3

e ♠ J 8
♥ K Q 8 6 4 2
♦ 10 7 2
♣ J 6

f ♠ K 8 4
♥ A 10 9 3
♦ K 8 7 2
♣ 9 4

2 What would you rebid on each of these hands?

	LHO	*Partner*	*RHO*	*You*
				1♠
	2NT	3♦	pass	?

a ♠ A Q 10 7 2
♥ K J 7 2
♦ 9 2
♣ A 4

b ♠ K J 10 9 2
♥ J 8 6
♦ A K 9
♣ 10 8

3 What would you rebid on these each of these hands?

	LHO	*Partner*	*RHO*	*You*
				1♥
	2NT	3♦	pass	?

a ♠ K 8 7
♥ A Q J 6 2
♦ J 9 3
♣ Q 4

b ♠ J 2
♥ A K Q 7 5
♦ A K 8
♣ 10 9 3

c ♠ 7 5
♥ K Q J 10 6
♦ A Q 6 5
♣ 7 5

d ♠ 9
♥ A K J 8 7
♦ A J 6 2
♣ K 6 4

ANSWERS

1 **a** 3♠ With a good spade suit, this hand is just right for 3♠, showing 6-9 points and long spades.

   b 3♥ To show a normal (6-9) raise to the two-level.

   c 3♣ Showing a hand worth at least a limit raise in hearts. You will bid game even if partner signs off in 3♥.

   d 3♦ At least five spades and 10+ points.

   e 4♥ Holding six-card support, you make your normal preemptive raise to game.

   f 3♣ This cuebid shows a limit raise or better of partner's hearts (10+ points). If partner bids only 3♥, you will respect his decision and pass.

2 **a** 4♠ Partner shows a hand worth a limit raise and you have enough to bid game.

   b 3♠ You have a minimum hand and no reason to expect game to be possible unless partner can bid again.

3 **a** 3♠ Partner shows 10+ points and spades, but you should sign off with your minimum hand. (The minor-suit honors are practically worthless.)

   b 4♠ You want to be in game somewhere. Although partner may hold only five spades, game in spades is the best bet. You can hardly bid 3NT with no club stopper.

   c 3♥ Nothing really appeals, but this shows a minimum hand and no spade support.

   d 3NT With extra values and good stoppers in both minors, 3NT looks best.

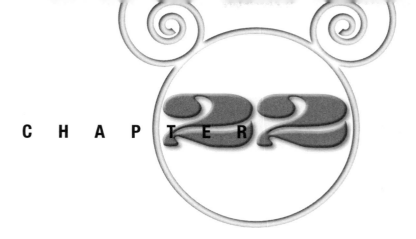

C H A P T E R 22

SOS AND OTHER REDOUBLES

WHAT'S IN A NAME?

When you redouble for rescue, this is known as an SOS Redouble. That's because **SOS (Save Our Souls)** is the international code transmitted by a vessel in distress. In the same way, a bridge player whose partnership is heading for a large penalty may also send out a distress signal.

Back in the deep mists of time, the original meaning of a double was that you thought the opponents had strayed out of their depth and you wanted to increase the penalty — all doubles were 'penalty doubles', in other words. As the years went by, it was found that in many situations it was better to play a double for takeout.

In this chapter we are going to look at redoubles. As with the double, the original meaning was a simple one — that you thought you had not strayed out of your depth and were therefore quite happy to redouble the stakes. Again it was decided as the years went by that there were many situations where it was beneficial to assign a different meaning to the redouble. In this chapter we will look at three of them: the SOS redouble, the lead-directing redouble and the redouble of a cuebid. Since it will be necessary to distinguish these from the standard type of redouble, let's take a look at that first.

The standard uses of redouble

In this section we will look at the main situations where you redouble to show strength. The most important of these is when partner's opening bid has been doubled for takeout. Suppose you hold this hand:

♠ 2 ♥ K J 10 6 ♦ A Q 8 4 3 ♣ J 8 2

LHO	Partner	RHO	You
	1♠	dbl	redbl

You redouble to tell your partner that your side has the majority of the points and that there is a good chance you can collect a worthwhile penalty from the opponents. The precise meaning of your redouble here may vary depending on your exact system, but it will promise 10+ points or so, and probably shows a hand with no fit for partner's suit. On this hand, you will be willing to double 2♦ or 2♥ yourself. By announcing that you are looking for a penalty, you give your partner the chance to double the opponents in 2♣.

A redouble has the same, strong, meaning in this auction:

LHO	Partner	RHO	You
	1NT	dbl	redbl

The redouble is for business. You are telling your partner that your side has more points than the opponents. You expect a contract of 1NT redoubled to succeed. If one of the opponents chooses to run, you are inviting your partner to double if he has something in the trump suit.

The situation remains the same when the opening bid is a preempt:

LHO	Partner	RHO	You
	3♥	dbl	redbl

One of the purposes of your partner's preempt was to put the opponents under pressure, to make them guess whether they should enter the auction or not. Your redouble tells partner that RHO has guessed wrongly! He has entered the auction and found a powerful hand sitting over him.

Partner has already described his hand, with the preempt. In no circumstances should he rebid 4♥. If LHO passes, partner should pass. If instead LHO bids, partner should pass or double. The opponents are in big trouble and it would be a serious mistake for partner to rebid his hearts, thereby preventing your side from collecting 800 or 1100!

The other use of a strength-showing redouble arises when a contract at the game level or higher has been doubled for penalties. A redouble then is natural – it means that you think the contract can be made.

This is a typical situation:

♠ K 2   ♥ A 9   ♦ K 10 8 4 3   ♣ A K J 2

LHO	Partner	RHO	You
			1♦
pass	2NT (11-12)	pass	3NT
dbl	pass	pass	redbl

LHO has some good diamonds sitting over you and thinks that 3NT will go down after a diamond lead. With a massive 18-count, you are confident that 3NT can be made anyway. You express this opinion with a redouble.

So much for the traditional type of redouble. Let's look now at a very different type of redouble, one that is for takeout!

The SOS Redouble

You would normally be happy to play in a doubled contract that was successful, particularly when you have been doubled into game. Suppose the opponents double you in 2♥, which will therefore be game if the contract is made. Even if a redouble were strength-showing, it would usually not be very sensible to make this call. By warning the opponents that you think the contract will succeed, you will make it attractive for them to escape into their own best contract, greatly improving their score.

Most players therefore have this agreement:

**When a partscore in a trump suit has been doubled
for penalties, a redouble is 'SOS'.**

An SOS Redouble asks partner to escape into another suit. Such a meaning is much more useful than the natural one. Suppose you hold these cards:

♠ 9 7 2   ♥ K 10 9 8 2   ♦ Q J 7 6 2   ♣ —

LHO	Partner	RHO	You
1♠	2♣	pass	pass
dbl	pass	pass	?

Partner has overcalled 2♣ and LHO has then reopened the bidding with a takeout double. RHO, who presumably has a stack of clubs sitting over your partner, has passed the double for penalties. It's not a pleasant situation and you can expect your partner to go at least two down. Although it is no certainty, you can probably do better in one of the red suits. Which one should you choose?

You don't want to make the choice, do you? For one thing, you want partner to play this hand – that's the least he deserves after his presumably poor overcall! Seriously, you want your partner to choose the better of his red suits and you can achieve precisely this aim by making an SOS Redouble. The redouble asks partner to escape into one of the unbid suits.

Why is a redouble in this situation SOS? Because it is a redouble of a part-score in a suit. If you thought partner could make 2♣ doubled, you would be content to pass, scoring well on what appears to be a partscore deal.

It's easy enough to remember that a redouble of a partscore in a suit is for takeout. What is not so easy is to judge when it is worthwhile attempting to rescue a partner who has just been doubled in some low contract. Your general strategy will depend on the type of overcall that your partner tends to make. If he is a sound character such as a bank manager, you can probably rely on his overcalls and should tend to leave the contract alone. If your partner is less disciplined and likes to overcall at the two-level on moderate five-card suits, you may do better to redouble and seek a less costly spot elsewhere.

The lead-directing redouble

The earlier book in this series, *25 Bridge Conventions You Should Know*, covered the topic of lead-directing doubles:

LHO	Partner	RHO	You
1♦	1♠	2♠	dbl

RHO's 2♠, a bid in the opponent's suit, shows at least a limit raise of diamonds. (A direct raise to 3♦ would have been preemptive.) What does your double of the 2♠ bid mean? If you had reasonable values and three or four spades, you would raise to 3♠ or 4♠ at this stage. Your actual double means that you are not strong enough to raise spades but you would still like a spade lead. Typically you will hold ♠A-x or ♠K-x. It's a very useful call. The opener may well be about to bid some number of notrump and it will then be essential, from your viewpoint, to get a spade lead.

Suppose instead that this is how the auction goes:

LHO	Partner	RHO	You
1♦	1♠	2♠	pass
3NT	all pass		

Partner will take note of the fact that you did not double the spade cuebid. If his spades are not particularly robust, he may try his luck by leading a different suit.

You will not fall off your chair when you hear that you can use a redouble to convey the same meaning when partner's overcall has been doubled (a negative double, for takeout). Suppose you have these cards:

♠ A 2   ♥ 8 4 2   ♦ J 10 6 2   ♣ 10 9 5 2

LHO	Partner	RHO	You
1♣	1♠	dbl	redbl

You do not have enough to raise spades but you would like a spade lead if LHO eventually plays the contract. Perhaps your partner's suit is headed by the king-jack and he would normally look elsewhere for his lead against a contract of, say, 4♥. After your redouble he will not hesitate to lead a spade.

Redouble of a control-showing cuebid

When an opponent doubles a control-showing cuebid, you and your partner will have an opportunity to redouble. What does such a call mean? The generally accepted method is this:

**When the partner of the cuebidder redoubles, he shows
a first-round control in the suit.**

**When the cuebidder redoubles, he indicates that
his control is first-round, rather than second-round.**

Here's an example:

	Partner		You
	♠ A K J 10 8 6 2		♠ 9 7 3
	♥ —		♥ K 10 2
	♦ 9 5		♦ A 8 6 4
	♣ A K Q J		♣ 9 8 5

LHO	Partner	RHO	You
	2♣	pass	2♦
pass	2♠	pass	3♠
pass	4♣	pass	4♦
dbl	pass	pass	redbl
pass	4NT	pass	5♣
pass	6♠	all pass	

Spades are agreed as trumps and the next two bids, 4♣ and 4♦, are ace-or-king cuebids (see Chapter 20). When LHO makes a lead-directing double of 4♦, partner passes so that you can clarify the nature of your diamond control. Since you have a first-round control, you redouble. This is enough to persuade partner to bid a small slam. Just in case you also hold the ♥A, which will provide a discard for the other diamond loser, partner bids RKCB on the way.

Suppose you had held the ♦K instead. How would the bidding have gone? Unable to redouble, to show first-round control, you would have cuebid your heart control next. Partner would then have signed off in 4♠, expecting to lose two diamond tricks when a diamond was led through dummy's king.

✓ There are two forms of the standard strength-showing redouble. When partner's opening bid is doubled, you may redouble to show the majority of the points and to invite partner to double any retreat. When a game contract is doubled, you may redouble to indicate confidence in your prospects.

✓ Any redouble of a partscore in a suit is SOS, for rescue.

✓ When partner's overcall has been doubled for takeout, you may redouble to say that you would like a lead of this suit. You should prefer to raise partner's suit if you have the playing strength to do so. A redouble therefore suggests A-x or K-x in partner's suit.

✓ If you play ace-or-king cuebidding (see Chapter 20), the cuebidder should redouble a doubled cuebid to show that he has first-round control rather than second-round control. Similarly, the cuebidder's partner can redouble a doubled cuebid to show that he holds first-round control of the suit.

SOS AND OTHER REDOUBLES

NOW TRY THESE...

1 What do you bid on each of these hands after this start to the auction?

LHO	Partner	RHO	You
1♥	2♣	pass	pass
dbl	pass	pass	?

a ♠ K J 7 6 5
♥ 8 2
♦ Q 10 7 6 5 4
♣ —

b ♠ Q 10 8 5
♥ J 7
♦ K J 8 7 3
♣ 6 2

2 Will you bid anything on these two hands?

LHO	Partner	RHO	You
1♥	2♣	dbl (neg.)	?

a ♠ K 5
♥ 9 8 6 2
♦ 10 7 5 4
♣ A 9 3

b ♠ Q J 5 4
♥ J 10 6 4
♦ 8 6 2
♣ K 3

3 You are investigating a slam when an opponent doubles your ace-or-king cuebid. What will you bid in each case?

LHO	Partner	RHO	You
	1♦	pass	1♠
pass	4♠	pass	5♣
dbl	pass	pass	?

a ♠ K Q 7 5 2
♥ 7 5 3
♦ K 5
♣ A 9 3

b ♠ A J 5 4 2
♥ J 7 5
♦ A 6 2
♣ K 3

ANSWERS

1 a redbl   Perfect for the SOS redouble! Given your void in clubs, diamonds or spades will almost certainly play better, and neither of these suits involves making more tricks than you are already committed to in clubs.

   b pass   This time you are likely to be in a 6-2 fit and there is no reason whatsoever to expect there is a better spot available in spades or diamonds. Partner could easily be 2-3-2-6, in which case any attempt at rescue will propel your partnership from the frying pan straight into the fire.

2 a 3♣   Do not redouble, for a lead, when you have the playing strength to raise. Use the redouble to say that you want partner to lead his suit even though you can't raise it.

   b redbl   You cannot raise the overcall with only K-x in clubs. You redouble to say that you would like a club lead against the opponents' contract.

3 a redbl   With first-round club control, you must redouble. If you make any other call, you are denying the ace of clubs.

   b 5♦   You would redouble with first-round club control. Here you have only a second-round control, so you continue to bid. It is still worth showing the diamond control because you will be declarer and therefore have no fear of two immediate club losers – a club lead will come up to your hand, not through it.

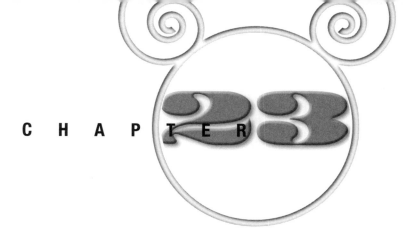

PICK-A-SLAM 5NT

WHAT'S IN A NAME?

♥ For many decades the meaning of a jump to 5NT was, 'Partner, please bid a grand if you hold two of the three top trump honors.' The convention was known as *Josephine* after the brilliant Josephine Culbertson. The modern Pick-a slam 5NT bid is used by many top partnerships including Larry Cohen and David Berkowitz.

The arrival of Roman Keycard Blackwood, which helps locate the trump king and queen, makes the traditional 'Josephine' meaning of 5NT largely redundant. This is particularly so if you also play Exclusion Blackwood (see Chapter 10). In this chapter we will look at a novel new use for the 5NT bid in slam auctions.

♠ 5 ♥ A J 8 2 ♦ A K 6 2 ♣ K Q J 2

Partner	You
1NT (15-17)	2♣
2♠	?

What do you bid now? You could just blast 6NT, but there's no guarantee that is the right spot. If only you had some bid that would say to partner, 'Do you have another four-card suit we could play in?' That's where the Pick-a-slam 5NT bid comes in.

How does Pick-a-slam 5NT work?

When you bid 5NT, and it has not been preceded by 4NT, you are asking partner to 'pick a slam'. Let's see how it works on our example hand:

Partner	You
♠ K Q 7 3	♠ 5
♥ K 3	♥ A J 8 2
♦ Q J 5	♦ A K 6 2
♣ A 9 8 4	♣ K Q J 2
1NT (15-17)	2♣
2♠	5NT
6♣	

You begin with Stayman, seeking a heart fit. What would most players do when they discovered that there was no 4-4 fit in a major? You're right — they would leap to 6NT. When the heart finesse lost and they went down, they would say, 'Sorry, partner, wrong slam. We can make 6♣.'

Playing 5NT as 'Pick-a-slam' enables you to bid the right slam. Your 5NT tells partner that there is no 4-4 spade fit and that you want to play in a small slam somewhere else. Now partner bids his other four-card suit: here, clubs. The 4-4 club fit comes to light and you pass. No need for anyone to say 'Sorry' now!

Here is a similar sequence:

Partner	You
♠ A Q 9 2	♠ K 8 3
♥ K 3	♥ A J 10 7 5
♦ K Q 9	♦ A J
♣ Q 10 8 3	♣ K J 4
1NT (15-17)	2♦
2♥	5NT
6NT	

You show your five-card heart suit with a transfer response and partner duly rebids 2♥. What now? Some players would jump to 6NT on your cards. That's not very sophisticated, is it? Partner might still hold four-card heart support, or three-card heart support and a ruffing value in one of the black suits. The better contract of 6♥ would then have been left behind. Other players would 'invent' a second suit, bidding 3♣ here, hoping to gather more information. A much clearer way of bidding this hand is to start with a transfer bid and then jump to 5NT, asking partner to pick a slam.

Which slams can partner choose? On this auction it is clear that you do not have your own second suit. If you did, you would have bid it on the second round. So, partner is being asked to choose between 6♥ and 6NT. With only two hearts he will obviously choose 6NT. Even if he held three hearts, he would probably choose 6NT unless he had a potentially useful ruffing value.

Let's change partner's hand a bit and give him a five-card minor:

Partner	You
♠ A Q 9	♠ K J 3
♥ K 3	♥ A 10 8 7 4
♦ K 9 3	♦ A J
♣ K 10 8 3 2	♣ A 9 4
1NT (15-17)	2♦
2♥	5NT
6♣	

With five clubs and only two cards in your heart suit, partner is entitled to suggest six of this suit as a final contract (even though he knows you do not hold four clubs). You have three-card club support and a ruffing value, so you are happy to accept the suggestion. Playing in clubs, you can ruff a diamond for an extra trick, making the slam comfortably unless there are two trump losers. You can see that 6NT is not such a good contract because you would usually have to rely on a finesse of the ♦J.

Let's look at a couple of 'Pick-a-slam' auctions that do not begin with a notrump bid. The first comes from a world championship (Bermuda Bowl) match played between USA and Italy.

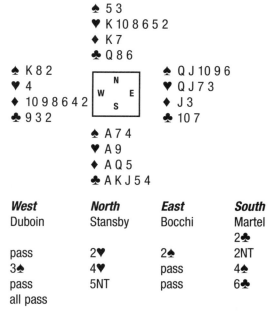

	♠ 5 3	
	♥ K 10 8 6 5 2	
	♦ K 7	
	♣ Q 8 6	
♠ K 8 2		♠ Q J 10 9 6
♥ 4		♥ Q J 7 3
♦ 10 9 8 6 4 2		♦ J 3
♣ 9 3 2		♣ 10 7
	♠ A 7 4	
	♥ A 9	
	♦ A Q 5	
	♣ A K J 5 4	

West	North	East	South
Duboin	Stansby	Bocchi	Martel
			2♣
pass	2♥	2♠	2NT
3♠	4♥	pass	4♠
pass	5NT	pass	6♣
all pass			

Martel's 4♠ was a cuebid with hearts agreed as the trump suit. Stansby was nervous about the quality of his hearts, however, so he bid a Pick-a-slam 5NT to look for a better spot. As on the previous auction, he could not hold four clubs (or he would have rebid 4♣ instead of 4♥ on the previous round). Martel would not therefore have bid 6♣ on a four-card club suit. Since he actually held five great clubs, he was happy to suggest a club slam. Stansby passed and twelve tricks were made with the aid of a spade ruff in dummy. The Americans thus brilliantly avoided the bad trump break waiting to destroy a slam in hearts.

Sometimes both players have a good suit of their own and it is a question of choosing between them. When the auction is uncontested, there is normally space to achieve this without any artificiality. It is different when the opponents enter with a preemptive bid:

	Partner		You
	♠ 10 4		♠ A K 9 8 6 3
	♥ A		♥ 10 6
	♦ A K 9 8 6 5		♦ J 7 2
	♣ A K 7 2		♣ Q 4

LHO	Partner	RHO	You
	1♦	4♥	4♠
pass	5NT	pass	6♦
all pass			

When partner hears of a good spade suit opposite, it is reasonable to hope for a small slam somewhere. Should diamonds be trumps or spades? He cannot tell and he consults you with a Pick-a-slam 5NT. Here you hold three-card diamond support. Since your spades are far from solid, you are happy to offer 6♦ as a possible contract and the par contract is reached. From partner's point of view, you might even have been able to bid 6♣, bringing a club fit to light.

Summary

✓ In certain auctions, a leap to 5NT can be used to mean, 'Please pick a slam, partner.'

✓ The bid is often used after a 1NT opening. Responder may start with Stayman or a transfer bid and then jump to 5NT to ask partner to choose a suitable slam contract.

✓ The bid may also be used when there is enough strength for a slam, but it is unclear which suit should be made trumps. If both players have a six-card suit, one may bid 5NT to ask partner to choose which suit should be trumps.

PICK-A-SLAM 5NT

NOW TRY THESE...

You are playing the Pick-a-slam 5NT bid (yes, partner persuaded you!). What would you bid next, in each of these auctions?

1   ♠ A K 8 3   ♥ Q 5   ♦ A J 8 7   ♣ A 6 2

LHO	Partner	RHO	You
	1NT (15-17)	pass	2♣
pass	2♥	pass	?

2   ♠ Q 7 2   ♥ 4   ♦ A K 9 8 2   ♣ A K Q 4

LHO	Partner	RHO	You
	pass	pass	1♦
pass	1♠	pass	3♣
pass	3♦	pass	3♠
pass	4♥	pass	?

How would you respond to partner's Pick-a-slam 5NT on each of these hands?

3   ♠ 7   ♥ A K 7 4   ♦ A K J 8 7   ♣ Q 7 3

LHO	Partner	RHO	You
		3♠	dbl
pass	4♣	pass	4♦
pass	5NT	pass	?

4   ♠ A 10 7 4   ♥ K Q   ♦ A 9 6 2   ♣ Q 7 3

LHO	Partner	RHO	You
			1NT
pass	2♦	pass	2♥
pass	3♣	pass	3NT
pass	5NT	pass	?

5   ♠ A J 5 3   ♥ A Q 6 4   ♦ K Q 7   ♣ A J

LHO	Partner	RHO	You
			2NT
pass	3♣[1]	pass	3♥
pass	5NT	pass	?

1.   Stayman.

PICK-A-SLAM 5NT

ANSWERS

1 **5NT** If partner had shown a four-card spade suit, you would have headed for a slam in the 4-4 fit there. It is not too late to discover such a fit! Bid 5NT, asking partner to pick a slam. If he suggests 6♦ or 6♠, you will pass. If he responds 6♣, this will be only a four-card suit (you have not denied four clubs yourself). In that case you will correct to 6NT.

2 **5NT** Partner's 4♥ bid is a cuebid, suggesting a slam. You are happy to accept, with your array of high cards, but cannot tell whether spades or diamonds will make the better trump suit. Bidding 5NT asks partner to choose a small slam. Opposite a passed hand, you have no realistic chance for a grand slam.

3 **6♣** Partner does not hold four hearts, since he would surely have responded 4♥ instead of 4♣ in that case. After you have shown a very powerful hand, by doubling and changing the suit, he is asking you to choose between the minor suits. Your clubs are strong enough to agree to play in his club suit.

4 **6♥** Partner has shown five hearts and four clubs (with 5-5 shape, he could have rebid 4♣ over 3NT). Since you have no primary fit for either of his suits, you would normally bid 6NT at this stage. However, you have only a single stopper in both spades and diamonds. This looks like the moment to play in a 5-2 heart fit. You can expect partner's hearts to be reasonable, since he has offered them as a possible trump suit even though he knows you hold only two hearts.

5 **6♠** Partner surely holds four spades, otherwise there would be no point in bidding Stayman. (Even if this inference were not present, you would bid 6♠ because 5NT has asked you to suggest a playable slam.)

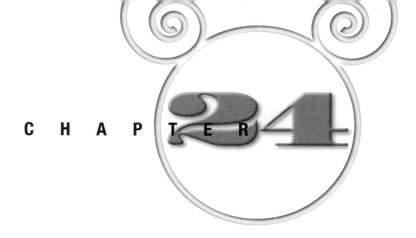

C H A P T E R **24**

SNAPDRAGON DOUBLES

 The Snapdragon Double was first publicized by *Jeremy Flint* in his book *Tiger Bridge* (1970). At that time he used the term for a wider range of what are now known as competitive doubles. Today, the Snapdragon Double has the specific meaning outlined in this chapter. The origin of its delightful name, however, remains a mystery.

This convention has a splendid name — one so good that you can almost justify playing the Snapdragon Double for the name alone. Is the convention a good one, too? We think so, and it is certainly widely played. As always, the decision is up to you. See what you think by the end of the chapter.

What is a Snapdragon Double?

Let's start with an example. You are sitting in the fourth seat with this hand:

♠ A Q 10 8 7 ♥ Q 3 ♦ 8 3 ♣ Q 8 7 3

LHO	Partner	RHO	You
1♦	1♥	2♣	?

What do you say? In the absence of any convention some players would risk supporting the heart overcall on just two trumps. The problem with bidding 2♠ instead is that it carries you past the safety level of 2♥, if partner is short in spades. The Snapdragon Double solves all your problems. You double and pass these messages to your partner:

(a)   I have enough strength to compete at this level

(b)   I hold at least five cards in the unbid suit (here, spades)

(c)   I have tolerance for your suit — at least a doubleton honor.

Have you ever made such an eloquent double? Not bad, is it? As you see from this example, a big advantage of the convention is that you can show length in a particular suit without having to risk bidding it at a dangerously high level. If partner has no liking for spades, he can dive for cover in 2♥, because you've said you can stand that.

This is the basic convention:

When the auction starts with three consecutive players bidding a new suit,
a double by the fourth player shows length in the fourth suit
plus tolerance for his partner's suit.

You can also use the convention when you have primary support for partner's minor suit and want to see if there is a fit in a major that you hold (because game will be easier in the major). Suppose you hold these cards:

♠ J 6 3   ♥ A K 8 7 3   ♦ 4   ♣ K 10 7 3

LHO	Partner	RHO	You
1♦	2♣	2♠	?

What now? You could raise clubs, yes, but perhaps partner has heart support. If instead you bid 3♥, and partner rebids 4♣, you won't know whether to go on or not. It is better to launch your hand with a Snapdragon Double.

A double at this level will carry the bidding as high as 3♥, when partner has a heart fit and a minimum hand. It follows that the double shows fair values. When partner does hold heart support he should be willing to show this, even over a raise to 3♠ by LHO.

How much are you giving up by using such doubles in an artificial way? Almost nothing! The 2♠ bid in the above auction is usually played as forcing. In that case it would be pointless to make a penalty double of the bid. If the opponents treat 2♠ as non-forcing, there may be some value in a penalty double. Not much, though, and the Snapdragon double is more useful. It would be awkward to play two different meanings for a double, depending on whether the third player's bid was forcing. Our advice is to adopt the Snapdragon Double in this situation, whether or not the third player's bid is forcing.

When you hold a very strong suit of your own, you may prefer to bid it directly, rather than suggesting tolerance for partner's suit at the same time.

♠ K Q J 10 8 4 ♥ A 3 ♦ 8 2 ♣ J 9 4

LHO	Partner	RHO	You
1♥	2♣	2♦	?

You are happy to play in spades, even if partner has one spade and six clubs. So, bid 2♠ here instead of making a Snapdragon Double.

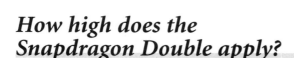

How high does the Snapdragon Double apply?

You may already play competitive doubles. In that case you can play the Snapdragon Double, which is in fact a variety of competitive double, up to the same level. If you have no such agreement to follow, it is reasonable to play all such doubles through 3♠. Suppose you hold this hand:

♠ 5 2 ♥ K Q 10 8 7 2 ♦ J 10 4 ♣ A 3

LHO	Partner	RHO	You
1♣	3♦	3♠	?

Partner's 3♦ overcall is weak. Even so, you may have a playable contract in hearts. When partner has length in hearts, you might eventually want to sacrifice in one of the red suits. Your best move at this stage is to show your heart length and diamond tolerance. You do this with a Snapdragon Double of 3♠. When the bid is made at such a high level, it is much more likely that your support for partner's suit is three cards rather than a doubleton. That's because you will need to play in his suit, at a fairly high level, if he has no support for your long suit. Partner will be well placed to judge the prospects for a sacrifice, should opener raise to 4♠ at his next turn.

How does partner bid facing a Snapdragon Double?

Partner has a fair picture of your hand when you enter with a double after three suits have been bid. You will typically hold five or six cards in your suit and two or three cards in his. The higher the level, the more likely it becomes that you have longer holdings and good playing strength.

If the original opener passes over your double, it will usually be fairly obvious to your partner which suit he should choose. Judgment will be required only when partner has values to spare and there is a question of bidding beyond the minimum level. The same judgment will be needed if opener has raised the ante by making a further bid himself. Partner will have to decide whether a further bid is justified in one of the partnership's suits.

Let's look at a couple of typical situations, to see the type of decision the original overcaller may have to make:

♠ K 10 5   ♥ 8 2   ♦ A K Q 8 3   ♣ J 5 4

LHO	Partner	RHO	You
		1♠	2♦
2♥	dbl	3♥	?

Partner has shown club length and diamond tolerance. Would you make a bid at this stage?

You don't have to bid just because you have three-card support for partner's clubs. What will happen if you bid 4♣ now? LHO will probably stretch to bid 4♥, even if he was planning to pass. Your partner may then sacrifice in 5♣. You have three quite likely defensive tricks in your own hand, with partner's values to come. You don't want to encourage a sacrifice from your partner and should therefore pass 3♥.

The situation is different here:

♠ Q 10 5   ♥ 8   ♦ A 8 3   ♣ K Q J 9 8 3

LHO	Partner	RHO	You
		1♥	2♣
2♦	dbl	4♥	?

Of course you will bid 4♠; on a good day the contract might even make. You can see that your clubs will be of limited use in defense against a heart contract, whereas your hand will play splendidly in support of spades.

Can you pass a Snapdragon Double?

A Snapdragon Double is a form of takeout double. The opponents have bid two suits and your partner has asked you to choose between your long suit and his long suit. As with any sort of takeout double, there are occasions when you will do best to pass it out for penalties. It will not happen very often, though, because your trumps will lie under declarer rather than over him. Suppose you hold this hand:

♠ 5 ♥ A 10 8 2 ♦ J 9 4 ♣ A K Q 10 4

LHO	*Partner*	*RHO*	*You*
		1♦	2♣
2♥	dbl	pass	?

    You hold only one card in partner's spade suit and just five clubs rather than six. You also hold four reasonable hearts. At matchpoints, with the opponents vulnerable, you might be tempted to pass in the hope of picking up a valuable 200. Remember that LHO's 2♥ is (usually) forcing, though, so he was prepared to see the bidding climb higher. Even on this hand it is quite risky to attempt to defeat 2♥ doubled, and you should certainly bid 3♣ playing IMPs.

✓ A Snapdragon Double is a form of competitive (takeout) double. It arises when three consecutive players have each bid a different suit. A double by the fourth player shows length in the unbid suit and tolerance for partner's suit.

✓ The strength required varies according to the level of the bid. At the one-level, you might double on as little as 7 points. At the three-level, you need considerable playing strength to make the call.

✓ When responding to a Snapdragon Double you have to choose between partner's suit and your own. With considerable extra strength you can make a jump response.

SNAPDRAGON DOUBLES

NOW TRY THESE...

Playing the Snapdragon Double, what would you bid on each of these hands?

	LHO	Partner	RHO	You
	1♦	1♥	2♣	?

1
- ♠ A K J 7 6
- ♥ Q 7
- ♦ 10 5
- ♣ 9 7 3 2

2
- ♠ A K Q 9 8 2
- ♥ 10 3
- ♦ K 8 3
- ♣ 7 5

3
- ♠ Q 10 9 7 2
- ♥ J 5
- ♦ 7 3 2
- ♣ A 9 3

4
- ♠ A 7 6
- ♥ 3
- ♦ J 10 7 4
- ♣ A Q J 6 3

5
- ♠ A K J 8 4
- ♥ K 6 5
- ♦ 7 2
- ♣ J 6 3

6
- ♠ K J 9 8 4
- ♥ Q 9 3
- ♦ 8 5 4
- ♣ 10 4

How will you reply to partner's Snapdragon Double in each case?

	LHO	Partner	RHO	You
			1♥	2♣
	2♦	dbl	pass	?

7
- ♠ A 10 2
- ♥ 6
- ♦ J 9 2
- ♣ A K Q 9 6 4

8
- ♠ J 4
- ♥ Q 8 6
- ♦ A 9
- ♣ K Q 10 8 7 3

9
- ♠ K 8
- ♥ 9 3
- ♦ J 10 4 2
- ♣ A K J 10 5

10
- ♠ 9 3
- ♥ K 5
- ♦ A 2
- ♣ A K 9 7 6 4 2

ANSWERS

1 dbl   Perfect for Snapdragon. You are happy to compete at the two-level in whichever major suit partner chooses.

2 2♠   Here your spade suit is strong enough to bid on its own. You have no wish for partner to choose between the majors.

3 pass   You do not have the values to enter the auction at this stage. The previous player's 2♣ bid is nearly always treated as forcing. If the auction dies in 2♦, you will have an opportunity to double (for takeout) then.

4 pass   If a double was for penalties, you would be happy to double here. Since you are playing the Snapdragon Double, you cannot double here. Nothing much is lost because 2♣ is almost certainly forcing anyway. You will have a chance to double some higher contract later.

5 2♦   Here you hold K-x-x support for hearts and are happy to make that suit trumps. Show a good hand for hearts by cuebidding the opponents' suit.

6 2♥   On this fairly weak hand you are worth no more than a single raise of partner's suit.

7 4♠   You have excellent support for partner's spades and sufficient extra values to raise him to game.

8 3♣   Partner may hold only five spades, so you should prefer 3♣ to 2♠.

9 2♠   Here you have only five clubs. It is better to play in partner's suit, particularly as you will be a level lower.

10 3NT   Partner has shown club tolerance, which may be x-x-x or Q-x. Nothing is certain in this life but it is surely worth attempting 3NT.

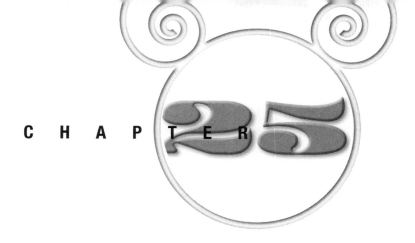

MULTI-COLORED TWO DIAMONDS

WHAT'S IN A NAME?

Terence Reese and *Jeremy Flint* gave birth to the Multi-colored Two Diamonds (known as 'Multi') in the late 1960s. Their intention was not to invent an opening that would be difficult to defend against; that was a bonus. Their purpose was constructive — to cover various hand types with one opening bid, thereby freeing up other opening bids for a new purpose. Hence the name — the 2♦ opening was used on many different types of hand.

When we looked at the Flannery 2♦ opening, way back in Chapter 2, we mentioned that many players prefer to use 2♦ as a natural weak two-bid. In this final chapter of the book we are going to describe a further possibility for the 2♦ opening — the notorious Multi-colored Two Diamonds. When first invented, it was banned by many authorities, who thought it would be too difficult a convention for opponents to counter.

There are many versions of the Multi, including several where the bid is used on both strong and weak hands of various types. Most of these are not allowed in competition in North America except at the highest levels. Here we will describe a fairly straightforward version, which can be used in most clubs and tournaments. You open 2♦ on either one of these hand types:

a weak two-bid in hearts, 6-10 HCP

a weak two-bid in spades, 6-10 HCP

'Why would you do this?', you may ask. There are two reasons why you might want to. First, to make things more difficult for your opponents, since they don't know which suit you have; second, because you want to use the 2♥ and 2♠ openings for something else.

The earlier book in this series, *25 Bridge Conventions You Should Know*, described the sort of hand that qualifies for a weak two-bid. You should hold a good six-card suit (usually containing two of the three top honors) and no four-card major on the side.

Having said that, it is only fair to add that some players do not restrict themselves to such guidelines. They open on poor suits, sometimes even on five-card suits. It is up to you to choose how disciplined a style you wish to adopt. We don't want to be accused of tempting you down a dubious path, so the examples we give of weak two-bids will be fairly traditional:

♠ A Q 9 8 5 2　♥ 8 3　♦ Q 9 4　♣ 10 6

You have 8 HCP and a highly respectable six-card spade suit. You would normally open a weak 2♠. Playing the Multi, you open 2♦ instead.

♠ 8　♥ K J 10 7 5 3　♦ Q 9 7 2　♣ 7 6

This hand does not qualify for a 3♥ opening, even thought you might be tempted at favorable vulnerability! Still, you do want to make life a little harder for the opponents so you open with a weak two-bid. Playing traditional weak two-bids, you open 2♥. Playing the Multi, you open 2♦.

If you are not already familiar with the Multi, you may think it will be difficult for responder to bid, not knowing which suit you hold. In fact it is remarkably easy, as we are about to see.

How do you respond to the Multi?

When you do not want to play at the game level, regardless of which suit partner has, you respond 2♥. Partner will pass this when he has a weak two-bid in hearts and correct to 2♠ when he has a weak two-bid in spades:

♠ K 7 2　♥ A 6　♦ K 10 7 2　♣ Q 8 7 2

Partner	You
2♦	?

You hold 12 HCP, not enough to make game opposite a weak two-bid, and should respond 2♥. Partner will pass when his suit is hearts. If instead he rebids 2♠, showing that his suit is spades, you will pass. Note that your 2♥ response does not promise any heart support at all. You are merely saying that if partner has a weak two-bid in hearts you do not want to bid any higher.

Suppose partner opens a Multi 2♦ and you can see chances of game if he holds spades but not if he holds hearts:

♠ A Q 8 3   ♥ 5   ♦ A 9 6 3   ♣ K J 10 6

Partner	You
2♦	?

Again you respond 2♥. You expect that partner is weak with hearts and in that case a contract of 2♥ will be high enough. If partner surprises you by rebidding 2♠, to show spades, you will re-evaluate your hand and raise to 4♠. (With a slightly weaker hand you could invite game by bidding 3♠.)

It is a little more complicated when you have good support for hearts but not spades:

♠ 6   ♥ A Q 9 5   ♦ K J 3   ♣ K 10 8 7 2

Partner	You
2♦	?

Strange as it may seem, you now respond 2♠. The meaning is, 'If your suit is spades, I do not want to go any higher. Please pass. If you have hearts, and will therefore have to rebid 3♥, I have a good fit for you and perhaps we can make game.' Indeed, opener should rebid 4♥ when he holds an upper-range weak two-bid (nearer 10 points than 6).

What if you hold a strong hand and may be able to make game whichever major suit partner holds? You then respond 2NT, an artificial inquiry bid that asks opener to describe his hand.

Partner	You
2♦	2NT

Opener rebids on these lines:

3♣	maximum weak two-bid with hearts
3♦	maximum weak two-bid with spades
3♥	minimum weak two-bid with hearts
3♠	minimum weak two-bid with spades

As responder, you will then be able to decide how high to play. Suppose partner opens with a Multi 2♦ and you hold this hand:

♠ A Q 7   ♥ K 2   ♦ A Q 7 2   ♣ Q 9 7 6

Partner	You
2♦	?

With 17 HCP, you may want to play in game. You start with the 2NT relay to discover what type of hand partner has. If he shows an upper-range hand,

you will play in partner's suit at the game level. If he shows a lower-range hand in spades, rebidding 3♠, you will take a gamble on 4♠ but it will be a close decision. The least encouraging response will be 3♥, lower-range with hearts, which you will pass. Ten tricks might be there but the odds are against it.

We have covered the important responding situations. Here's a summary:

	Partner 2♦	You ?

2♥	'Pass if you hold hearts'
2♠	'Pass if you hold spades, otherwise bid 3♥ or 4♥'
2NT	inquiry bid, as described above
3♣/3♦/3♥/3♠	natural and forcing, on a long and strong suit
3NT/4♥/4♠	to play

What happens when the Multi is doubled?

LHO	Partner 2♦	RHO dbl	You ?

There are a number of ways that people play this double, but however strong a hand it implies, it is always for takeout. You will want to raise the level of the preempt if you have a fit with partner, so most of your actions will try to do this, bearing in mind that you're not sure which suit partner has. As a result, for example, a response of 2♠ must still show good heart support, since you are forcing the bidding to the three-level if partner actually has hearts, and not spades. This is the best scheme after a double:

pass	nothing particular to say
redbl	you want to play in 2♦ redoubled
2♥	to play opposite hearts, willing to go higher in spades
2♠	to play opposite spades, willing to go higher in hearts
2NT	the usual enquiry bid
3♥/4♥	'Pass or correct': to play at this level in partner's long suit

This is a common situation:

♠ Q 10 7   ♥ K 9 2   ♦ K 8 6 5 2   ♣ 7 3

LHO	Partner 2♦	RHO dbl	You ?

You want to remove some bidding space from the opponents, who hold the balance of the points and doubtless a fit somewhere. You don't know which major partner holds but that is no problem. You respond 3♥, to play in partner's suit at the three-level. If his suit is spades, he will correct to 3♠. This is not a game try and partner is not invited to bid game — you are merely raising the barrier. If you were seriously interested in game, you would respond 2NT.

What happens when the Multi is overcalled?

When there is a two-level overall, you double to tell the opener to pass if the overcall is in his suit (you may see partner licking his lips!). Otherwise he should bid the major that he does hold. This would be a typical auction:

	Partner		*You*
	♠ A Q 9 7 6 3		♠ J 4
	♥ 7 5 2		♥ A 3
	♦ 9 7		♦ K J 6 2
	♣ J 4		♣ A 9 7 5 3

LHO	*Partner*	*RHO*	*You*
	2♦	2♥	dbl
pass	2♠	all pass	

With an opening bid of your own, you are unwilling to sell out to 2♥. Your double asks partner to pass if he happens to hold hearts, otherwise to bid 2♠. This is better than your having to 'guess' to bid 2♠ yourself, which could be disastrous if partner held hearts!

A double of a 2♠ overcall would have a similar meaning. Partner should pass with spades, otherwise rebid 3♥.

When the opponents overcall at the three-level, a double is for penalties. If you wish to play in three of partner's major after an overcall of 3♣ or 3♦, you respond 3♥. Partner will either pass this or correct to 3♠, depending on which suit he holds.

What do 2♥ and 2♠ openings mean now?

The 2♦ opening will cause plenty of problems for the opponents, who will not know which suit you hold. However, this is not the main purpose of the Multi, as we mentioned at the outset of this chapter. By covering two different hand types with one opening bid, you can now use the opening bids of 2♥ and 2♠ to have a different meaning from normal. For example, 2♥ can be Flannery, and 2♠ can be a minor two-suiter, or a weak preempt in an unspecified suit.

This is another popular scheme:

2♥   five hearts and a five-card minor, 6-10 HCP

2♠   five spades and a five-card minor, 6-10 HCP

So, you open 2♥ on a hand like this:

♠ 6   ♥ K Q 10 8 4   ♦ J 9 8 5 2   ♣ Q 5

If partner were particularly short in hearts and wanted to discover which minor you held, he would respond 2NT. You would rebid 3♦ in this case.

Summary

✓ The simplest version of the Multi 2♦ opening covers two hand-types: a weak two-bid in hearts and a weak two-bid in spades.

✓ The main responses are 2♥ (high enough if partner has hearts), 2♠ (high enough if partner has spades) and 2NT (an enquiry bid). Over 2♥ or 2♠, opener will pass or correct to his major.

✓ After 2♦ - 2NT, the opener rebids 3♣ with an upper-range weak two-bid in hearts, 3♦ with an upper-range weak two-bid in spades, 3♥ and 3♠ with lower-range weak two-bids.

✓ Opening bids of 2♥ and 2♠ may now be assigned new meanings. One popular scheme is that they represent hands of 6-10 HCP, with a five-card major and a five-card (unknown) minor.

MULTI-COLORED TWO DIAMONDS

NOW TRY THESE...

Playing the Multi, what would you open on each of these hands?

1	♠ A 9 6 3		**2**	♠ 7 6 3
	♥ K Q 10 8 7 3			♥ Q J 10 9 4 2
	♦ 7 2			♦ 8
	♣ 8			♣ K 9 2
3	♠ 9 6		**4**	♠ A K Q 9 8 5
	♥ K Q J 8 3			♥ 8 6 3
	♦ 7			♦ 4
	♣ J 10 6 4 2			♣ J 9 2

Partner opens a Multi 2♦. How will you respond on each of these hands?

5	♠ 10		**6**	♠ 9 2
	♥ A K 9 8			♥ —
	♦ J 9 6 2			♦ K Q J 9 7 2
	♣ A K 10 4			♣ 10 8 7 6 3
7	♠ Q 5		**8**	♠ A 6
	♥ K 5			♥ A Q 7
	♦ J 8 4			♦ A 9 6 2
	♣ A K 10 7 6 2			♣ Q 10 7 3

How will you respond to partner's enquiry bid on each of these hands?

You	Partner
2♦	2NT
?	

9	♠ K Q 10 8 7 3		**10**	♠ 10 2
	♥ 8 5			♥ Q J 10 5 3 2
	♦ K 10 3			♦ K 4
	♣ J 4			♣ 9 7 4
11	♠ 7		**12**	♠ A J 10 9 6 5
	♥ A Q 8 7 3 2			♥ 7
	♦ 9 4 3			♦ 9 5
	♣ Q 10 7			♣ J 10 8 3

ANSWERS

1   pass   You should not open any sort of weak two-bid with a four-card major on the side, and you are too light for a 1♥ opening.

2   2♦   With a decent suit, including three of the top five honors, and so little defense, you cannot miss an opportunity to make life awkward for the opponents.

3   pass   This is not a weak two-bid, unless you're very undisciplined (or aggressive). It would be perfect for a 2♥ opening, showing hearts and a minor, if you play that.

4   2♦   There is no point in advertising 6-10 HCP as your range for a weak two-bid if you then open 1♠ on hands like this, thinking 'I'm good enough for a one-bid.'

5   2♠   You expect partner to be weak with spades. If he surprises you by rebidding 3♥, you will raise to game.

6   pass   There is no law against passing when you are happy to play in diamonds!

7   2♥   You are not strong enough to respond 3♣. Playing at the two-level in partner's suit will be high enough.

8   2NT   You can see a fair chance of game and should ask what type of hand partner has.

9   3♦   This response shows an upper-range weak two-bid in spades.

10   3♥   Here you have a lower-range weak two-bid in hearts.

11   3♣   With 8 HCP you are in the middle of the range. All your points are working, however, and you have a singleton too. Treat this as an upper-range hand.

12   3♠   Nice shape and good intermediates, yes, but don't get carried away! With only 6 HCP you should describe it as a minimum and respond 3♠.